ADVANCE PRAISE FOR *MANNING UP*

"When I read a trans anthology I clamor for words and sentences which gird my sense of self and assist me in making my life more tangible. In other words, I long to be seen. As a trans man, I found myself reading *Manning Up* with a sense of pride, knowing these men have courage enough to allow us a glimpse into their lived experiences. It is no easy task...but these writers have done a superb job. A great way to thank the writer of great words is to buy their books, and I encourage all to do so."
  —Morty Diamond, Editor of *From the Inside Out: Radical Gender Transformation, FTM & Beyond* and *Trans/Love: Radical Sex, Love & Relationships Beyond the Gender Binary*

"It is the distinct tone of each story that gives this book its strength, separates it from 'coming out' books, and makes it accessible and compelling to anyone, not just people in the GLBT community...I'm not going to lie to you and say this is a book of quick and easy reads, of short essays about being a man in modern society. There are pieces in here that will challenge you. There are pieces that are poetic and lyrical and others that are forceful and in-your-face. They are not all uplifting, with pat endings, starring the characters that popular media has taught us to expect in the stories of trans* people. But they are worth your time."
  —JJ Vincent, *The Good Men Project* magazine

"After a recent episode of life grumbling where I found myself saying I'm sick of gender, gender, gender...I begrudgingly picked up *Manning Up* and began to read. Wow! I found myself crying, laughing, annoyed, proud, grieving and deeply touched. While *Manning Up* is about gender, the reality is that this book is about growing up and stepping up. This is a book that encapsulates the complexities of doing both. What so many of us experience on this gender journey—confusion, determination, compassion, ferocity, love—takes courage. The willingness of these contributors to be open and share from their hearts, to me, is the epitome of what it means to Man Up! I truly feel the courage of them all."

—Aidan Key, Gender educator, activist, and founder of Gender Odyssey

"Manning Up will create space for so many that have not been able to see themselves reflected in this way . . . This book will most certainly find its way into the gender studies cannons of many a school across the world."

—J Mase III, Author of *And Then I Got Fired: One Transqueer's Reflections on Grief, Unemployment & Inappropriate Jokes About Death*

First published 2014 by Transgress Press

Library of Congress Cataloguing in Publication Data

Manning Up: Transsexual Men Finding Brotherhood, Family and Themselves / Edited by Zander Keig and Mitch Kellaway

Copyright © 2014 Zander Keig and Mitch Kellaway

ISBN: 149749219X
ISBN: 9781497492196

Transgress Press, Oakland, CA

Manning Up

Manning Up

TRANSSEXUAL MEN ON FINDING BROTHERHOOD, FAMILY AND THEMSELVES

Edited by Zander Keig and Mitch Kellaway

Zander dedicates this book to:

*my wife Margaret Keig for bringing such immense joy to my life,
my father Rick Hermelin for his unconditional support,
and my friend Jamison Green for his impactful
and insightful mentorship.*

Mitch dedicates this book to:

*Jocelyn, the other half of my heart,
Harlan and Owen, the most supportive brothers a man could have,
my mother Barbara for always kindling my fire for books,
and my departed nana Alice, wherever you're looking on from.*

TABLE OF CONTENTS

IV
NEW TERRITORY

FOREWORD

Jamison Green

The traditional method of becoming a man involves the simple passage of time, the development of a somber consciousness of duty or responsibility, combined with the realization of the inner strength to live up to that responsibility. This method presumes a starting point of boyhood, an accident of birth through which male anatomy confers a specific destiny.

Those individuals born with the anatomy designated "male" may follow many different paths to live out their manly destiny: some may find an easy, or a direct (though not easy) route, others may drift far and wide before they connect with themselves; some may lose their way, remaining "irresponsible boys" all their lives. There are no guarantees. Male anatomy does not fulfill its promise automatically, so when it comes to the ability to "man up," there is no predicting which boys will find it in themselves to become the men that others might hope for them to be, or that they might aspire to be themselves.

Trans men face an extra set of hurdles. First is the female body in which they are born. The second is the invisibility of their masculinity—the adults around them cannot see who they are as children, and cannot imagine who they will become. The third—which is not universal for trans men, but is nevertheless common—is the actual visibility of their masculinity, when their peers (and some adults, perhaps) *do* see that they are not able to perform in a way that is acceptable for women.

Then there is the hurdle of our own self-perception, the limitations we impose upon ourselves through the ways we internalize the judgments of others, which often functions in concert with the limitations placed upon us through our access to information about how we might change our own circumstances. And, finally, assuming bodily modification is a necessity for some of us, there is the hurdle of practical access to transformative technologies. This is an extra set of hurdles that some people might say was none of our business, that we are not entitled to reach to overcome, even if we are capable of doing so.

The men represented in this anthology are some of the many who have met these challenges head on, who have struggled to find peace in their bodies and their place in the world. Some are men who would take on different labels, or who may reject traditional masculine conventions, and some are men who want nothing more than their innate maleness to be seen and reflected back to them.

They are men who—in their individual ways—incorporate a larger consciousness in their manning-up, a consciousness of life beyond maleness. They have faced the challenges of overcoming fear and shame, of confronting institutionalized gender stereotypes and prejudices from within and without in ways that most people never dream possible. They confront the difficulties inherent in trans-ness, and they exhibit the courage transsexual people are famous for: the courage to proceed on their own path to authenticity and self-acceptance.

Some people express doubts about transsexual people, doubts that imply we are deceitful, that we are engaged in masquerade, that we can "never be something we were not born to be"—in other words, they believe that the form of one's physical body at birth is the definition of that person's role in life. Some people believe that chromosomes define sex, and sex is what gives meaning to life by virtue of traditional divisions of labor and duties, which can never be escaped. Some people believe that there are aspects of the human condition that are essential, that can never be changed.

But if these beliefs were true, we—as human beings—would never strive to overcome adversity. We would never struggle against our limitations; we would never attempt to better ourselves, or to help others overcome what might seem to be insurmountable odds, like the much-admired battles against cancer and other diseases, or efforts to mitigate or create adaptations for congenital defects.

Just because one may not be able to relate readily to the transsexual person's struggle, that struggle is no less worthy than any other quest for human potential, inner peace, or connection with spirit. The predicament in which transsexual people find ourselves is as classic and universal as any other search for wholeness and meaning; it just takes its own, unique, unusual, sometimes dramatic form.

To "man up" can mean to take responsibility, to get tough, to "grow a pair"—all of which are euphemistic phrases for *being* a man, not just *acting like* one. What's the difference? As the men included in this collection attest, being a man involves knowing who you are and how you fit into the world of men. No man gains this knowledge automatically. It is a process for each of us, regardless of race, class or age.

The men who share pieces of their stories in these pages are in varying stages of this process. Their diverse backgrounds, ages and racial heritage illuminate their journeys, and their histories of physical and socio-cultural obstacles enrich their appreciation of the nuances involved in taking their places among the men in their spheres, as well as redefining their relationships with women. And their awareness of their transsexual status, while central for some, is never far from the surface for any of these men, as they reflect on their situations and their passages.

Naturally, it is transsexual experience that distinguishes these men's manning up. One might ask: how can these men manage both the process of transition from female-to-male and the process of discerning and becoming the kind of man one aspires to be, when many men never manage the manning up process alone? The answer to that "how" question is quite individual, different for each man, but I predict the answers would be similar in the perspective each of them has by virtue of coming from an "outsider" position—not that they would see the same things, but that they would see *something* at all.

That they can manage this is only one of the factors that distinguish transsexual men from their non-transsexual peers, but it is a factor that could speak volumes about the social construction and biological nature of gender and sex that our culture has barely begun to observe, let alone define or understand. Since the number of published accounts of masculine transitions can as yet be tallied without breaking far into double digits, these essays are still among the vanguard, the first known explorations of this aspect of human experience. As such, they are sometimes raw, sometimes tentative, and always brave.

Some say that in a perfect world no one would need to transition. We would all be able to manifest and be respected for our best selves, no matter what kind of body we might have: maleness or femaleness would not define us, and we would not be prisoners of gender roles or power games; no one would have to be ashamed of their sexuality; no prejudice would confine us. But in spite of the limitations of language describing the feelings that underlie a transsexual transition, I do not think any of these utopian projections would eliminate the need some people have to change their bodies.

Well, I confess, first of all, that I don't think these utopian visions could possibly come to pass in the lifetime of anyone living as I write this. Some might call this a failure of my imagination. But I have more confidence in the depths of the human body and the richness of the human psyche that is enmeshed with that body, even though we can't yet explain it.

I trust my own experience, and that of my brothers whose words reach out through this book to find an audience of equal explorers who, whether or not they themselves are transitioners or trans people of any variation, are able to appreciate the profound and intrepid quests these men are undertaking, and glean from them fresh insights.

INTRODUCTION

Zander Keig and Mitch Kellaway

Transition Is Only the Beginning of Our Stories

This anthology has been our labor of love, originally sparked at Gender Odyssey 2007 in Seattle, Washington. Zander was in attendance that year and, despite how educational and affirming the conference could be, had been left feeling there needed to be more venues for trans men to openly discuss lived experiences of manhood. Already an anthologist (*Letters for My Brothers: Transitional Wisdom in Retrospect*, 2011), he knew one way to address his concern was to invite men to write about their lives.

Six years later, he found a ready collaborator in Mitch, a writer from across the country. After a flurry of emails, we finally met face-to-face at the Philadelphia Trans Health Conference in 2013. Our collaboration, as two trans men a generation apart, comes through in the finished collection, which has an unprecedented span of generational voices—something we're particularly proud of, in addition to its diversity of racial, class, sexual and spiritual experience.

Over the year we've spent co-editing, this project has been constantly girded by a simple belief: trans people telling their own stories can be both a profoundly healing and revolutionarily defiant act. When space is made for presenting transition narratives within the wider context of an individual's life, complex, heartwarming and rawly human tales emerge. And, just as the essays that follow present diverse experiences of what it means to be *human*, they also present divergent understandings of what it means to be a *man*, be *trans* and be a *trans man* (or trans* man, transman, transsexual man, transgender man or FTM)—three distinct, though interrelated, identities.

Transition is rarely the endpoint of one's story, as pop culture or mass media might have us believe. Rather, it is the beginning of something new for every man who goes through it, whether he considers himself post-transition or in a constant state of gender change.

The twenty-seven men who've generously contributed their stories to this anthology give insight into how transition offers expanded understandings of embodied masculinity, new feelings of brotherhood and community, a fresher self-image slate, unfamiliar experiences of privilege and bias, emergent roles in families and friendships and unknown, growth-inspiring challenges yet to face.

A Reader's Guide

The topics of the following essays intermingle, reflecting the messiness and intricacy of lives being lived. Even so, we've done our best to group essays together to allow readers a more sustained interaction with the overarching themes of finding oneself, family and community.

In "**Part I: Manning Up**," C. Michael Woodward, Shaun LaDue, Loren Cannon, Ezekiel Reis Burgin, Rayees Shah, C.T. Whitley and Daniel Vena address not simply how they've physically embodied maleness, but how they've worked and matured towards being the particular men they desire to be.

In "**Part II: Family Man**," Aaron H. Devor, Willy Wilkinson, Nathaniel Ezekiel, Chad Ratner, Gus, and Emmett Troxel discuss their familial roles as fathers, husbands, grandfathers, boyfriends and sons—including thoughts on newfound love and intimacy, the anxieties and triumphs of disclosure and second chances at realities once considered lost.

In "**Part III: Men Like Me**," A. Scott Duane, Trystan T. Cotten, Gavin Wyer, Mitch Kellaway, H. Adam Ackley, Dustin Ashizz and Brice

D. Smitth tell us what they've gained through being in communities with other men.

In "**Part IV: New Territory**," Jack Sito, James C.K., lore m. dickey, Ryan K. Sallans, Max Wolf Valerio, Lance Cox and Micah nuance understandings of male privilege, traditional masculinity, labels and "passing," while addressing the big pictures of journeying towards happiness, meaning and peace.

One can often hear trans men, in rightful pride, referring to ourselves as "self-made." There is so much truth in that word—of the fortitude and grit it takes to be oneself in a world where that is too often held out of reach. Yet at the same time, the phrase evokes an image of a man cut free from a network, forging ahead solo. Sometimes—in truth, too often—this may be an immediate reality.

But gender transition is hardly a one-shot deal. It would sell the stories of our lives, loved ones, social webs and communities short if we presented it as static and disconnected. Transition is a dynamic process, one that moves us both closer to a comfortable resting place even while shifting, often happily, our locations and meanings within life's many roles and relations. No self-made man is forged in a vacuum, and every self-made man needs someone to lean on now and again.

Zander Keig
Berkeley, CA

Mitch Kellaway
Somerville, MA

PART I
MANNING UP

MANNING UP

C. Michael Woodward

Unlike the messages I got from my lesbian separatist community, transitioning is not about copping out or defecting to the enemy camp, seeking privilege or attention, or running from oppression. It's not about hiding, and it's *definitely* not about drama. Transitioning is about personal integrity: the resolve to be myself no matter what. Figuring out who that "self" actually is has been the most challenging and rewarding aspect of my transition.

Fifteen years ago, before the epiphany of my trans identification, I didn't really have a "self" to be; I was definitely making it all up as I went along. I came of age in the late 1970s in a small, central Indiana town, before the Internet and cable television existed. We were a middle-class, white Protestant family and, like most everyone else I knew, we spent a lot of time at church. I shrugged skeptically at all the excitement over some ancient storybook, but I went along with it year after year. I didn't realize there were other options; it was just what we did.

I shrugged skeptically at femininity, too. I was a chubby, awkward tomboy. I had plenty of intelligence, but my social and physical inelegance did me no favors. Nonetheless, I struggled desperately to fit in. I tried so hard to be the beauty queen my mom wanted me to be that I even competed in a Junior Miss pageant. I really wanted to win—to please my mom and impress my classmates. I failed miserably at all of it, though, and it showed. The only limited conclusion I could come to was that I wasn't comfortable in anything that didn't have pockets.

As early as elementary school, I started telling tales about myself that weren't completely true. Nothing major, just a few fibs about my ancestry or stories about trips I'd never really taken or dreams I'd never actually had. I pretended to be into the same movies, music or boys my friends were. Like Sally Field at the Oscars, I just wanted people to like me. As I grew, the embellishments and exaggerations became habitual. The duplicity was never malicious; it was just what I did. That doesn't mean I didn't hurt anyone along the way.

In my twenties, I fancied myself a knight in shining armor, rescuing damsels in distress and slaying whatever dragons needed slaying. There were a lot of distressed damsels over the years. This one's car broke down. That one wanted to escape from a relationship gone bad. This one, well, she wasn't particularly attractive, but she was lonely and needed a friend.

I was a charismatic chameleon, donning whatever truth was needed to impress or persuade. I even shoplifted a time or two because I didn't want to disappoint my kleptomaniac girlfriend. I was proud of the number of notches on my bedpost; it meant they liked me. Still, if there were any women (or, occasionally, men) I didn't cheat on or lie to about something or other, it was only because we weren't together long enough.

My proclivity for perpetuating falsehoods was taking a toll. My life was a mess. I lived on fast food, had a sedentary job and home life, never got enough sleep, smoked heavily, drank too much too often and was a hundred or more pounds overweight. I wasn't just lazy—I went out of my way to avoid a healthy lifestyle. I call this my "passively suicidal" period: I baited the diabetes that runs in my family and the lung cancer that killed my father at age forty-six. I knew I was a ticking time bomb, and I didn't give a flying fuck. "I mean, really, what is the point?" I asked myself on a number of occasions. "We're all going to die anyway. Why bother?"

I wanted to believe just about anything was true except my own reality. By my mid-thirties, I had no idea where I was going or what

I would do if and when I ever got there. I just knew I could not keep doing what I'd been doing for the first three decades. I hated my (really great corporate) job, I resented my (wonderful, loving) lesbian partner and I wanted nothing to do with anything about my comfortably dispassionate life. I was always looking for someone or something new to take me away.

After eight years together, I abruptly walked out on my wife and our freshly custom-built suburban home without much forethought or explanation. I could no longer bear exposing her or anyone else to the shameful monster I believed myself to be. With absolutely no idea what to do next, I set up camp on a friend's couch and contemplated my fate.

———

Standing in line for the ladies' room at the local women's bar a month later, I find myself staring at a copy of *The Word*, Indiana's gay newspaper. On the front page is an article about a gay-friendly workshop promising to help you get your life out of a rut. Intrigued, I wave several women past me in line so I can keep reading. "Interesting timing," I think as I tuck the paper into the pocket of my leather jacket and proceed to take care of business in the restroom.

As I reclaim my perch at the bar, I notice a pretty young thing smiling at me. She's a hot one, but I'm too distracted to return the pass tonight. I finish my drink quickly and fish out a tip for Marge-in-Charge, our resident bartender-slash-smartass. I say goodnight to my fellow bar-flies and drive home, uncharacteristically alone and sober, and lost in thought.

The next morning, I re-read the article. I am being invited to live more passionately and powerfully. There's a session coming up the following weekend in Cincinnati, less than two hours away. *It sounds really good, but would it actually help someone like me?* I decide to call the "For More Information" number. Instantly and effortlessly, I connect to a sweet, gentle male voice.

"You'll surely benefit from the program no matter where you are in life," he assures me. "I know I did. If you were curious enough to get this far, you most definitely won't regret making the trip to Cincinnati."

Everything he says to me feels exactly right, and I decide to accept his invitation. A few days later I find myself signing in at the registration table for a workshop called, "The Experience." And boy, does it live up to its name.

The Experience turns out to be a confidence-building "personal empowerment" program built back in 1978 by, for and about queer folks. While its essence is rooted in EST, another popular "transformational" program of the era, The Experience presents concepts specifically through a gay-and-lesbian lens. Participants are coached in healing the inescapable psychological harms of discrimination, oppression, bullying and shaming of queer people that permeate our society.

I'm here with twenty-three other people from all over the country. Walking in, my imagination revels in the anonymity of the situation. *Not one of them knows me or anything about me. If ever there was a chance to be anyone I wanted to be, this is definitely it. I'll lay it on thick—go for the Oscar!* Then another, quieter voice reminds me that I've come here for a reason, and I'll only get out of this opportunity whatever I decide to put into it. Already a moment of truth and the workshop has only just begun.

Over the next two-and-a-half days, program facilitator Honey Ward leads each of us through a variety of touchy-feely activities with the whole group, smaller sections, or alone. A master at her craft, she helps each participant to peel away, like onion skins, the emotional scars that have accumulated.

When we're through, I leave with the realization that I had arrived in Cincinnati a lost and broken soul lacking any insight into how that came to be. Now I know that there's no shame in being exactly who I am, whoever that is. I deserve unconditional love, and "what other people think of me is none of my business." I can allow myself permission to forgive my past missteps and I possess the tools to deal with their repercussions.

For the first time, the positive energy running through me feels stronger than the negative. Having never taken a shine to the whole "God" thing, this program is the closest I've ever come to a religious experience. Though my friends quip that I've joined a cult, I know it's not like that. I'm on a quest. I've discovered new dragons to slay: the ones in my own mind. I don't have all the answers to who I am or why I am how I am, but I know that I'm on the right track.

———

Despite my awakening, old habits die hard. Two months later, I'm still struggling with behaving authentically, but I'm growing incrementally more adept. I enroll in a second Experience workshop called The Intensive, and on the second day I experience a much-needed expansion on my worldview. Our facilitator instructs us to craft "vision statements" for our lives. For several hours, we individually work on synthesizing what we've learned from previous self-explorations into one mission-driven sentence meant to guide our every waking moment from now to eternity. We're going to reconvene in the afternoon to share our vision statements with the whole group.

I'm thrilled. I have this writing project nailed: I'll produce a perfect, meticulously-worded vision statement that will impress everyone with its insightful crafting. I'll be universally praised and affirmed, and everyone will like me. I figure I can fudge a little on the actual content in favor of rhythm and flow, as long as I weave in all the right empowerment lingo.

But as the term "personal empowerment" suggests, it's this quest for props-over-purpose that finally challenges my integrity-compromising behavior in a way I ultimately can't ignore. I spend the assigned hours staring at the blank page in front of me. I know in my heart what I need to say, but it isn't what the rest of me wants to write. I'm just too ashamed.

So instead I sigh and shift uncomfortably in my chair. I look around the hotel lounge at the other participants sitting in their own worlds, looking pensive or frustrated. One woman scribbles madly in her journal, tears in her eyes, smiling ear-to-ear. Others chat quietly in pairs or threesomes, taking advantage of the downtime to relax.

As the clock ticks away, I drum my pen nervously on my notebook. Whatever I'm going to say, it has to be something I'm willing to be held accountable for—I'm just not sure I'm ready for that. Then something happens: when I finally put pen to paper, the words seem to write themselves, almost without my consent. After a moment, I lay the pen down on the table and take in my new vow:

My vision is to always seek the truth within myself and others, and to listen and respond to what that truth is saying; to communicate honestly, openly and lovingly to every person who touches my life, including myself.

Listening. That's what I need to do. If I can just quit opening my mouth to fill the silence and start paying closer attention to my inner voice, I'll find the lightness I've been craving.

I don't have to listen very long to hear new information. The day after we craft our vision statements, we're treated to a "makeover": a fresh look to help project our newly harnessed personal power. We get quite the spa treatment. I watch as some have their hair colored or cut and others try out bold new glasses. Then we all select high-quality clothes, borrowed from the organization's donated collection, to debut at that night's celebratory banquet.

However, my ample body can only fit into two of the women's outfits—and I hate them both. The well-meaning volunteers all insist I look fabulous in the green-and-purple knit pant suit, but I feel like a clown. After a good fifteen minutes of trying to explain something I have no language to describe, I finally snap.

"Look, this is supposed to be about what makes me feel *powerful*, right? Screw this! You want me to feel powerful? Gimme a god-damned TIE!"

There it is: I've asked for what I need. Instead of going along with what everyone else tells me I should want, do, be or think, *I* make the call. And it shocks me as much as it does the poor volunteers. After a few moments of uncomfortable silence, they look around at each other and back at me. And then, they smile. None of us are quite sure what it all means, but it feels like a real breakthrough.

That night, I attend the celebration in a silk, deep mustard-colored men's dress shirt with a muted brown-and-burgundy striped tie, a tank top in place of a bra and the decidedly masculine-looking loafers and slacks I'd brought with me. In the spirit of theater, I agree to a bit of light powder and blush, but not without some trepidation. Though it certainly isn't the first time I've worn a tie, it *is* the first time I've done so from a place of personal strength and with unconditional support. While I had generally never embraced what I considered "feminine" self-descriptors, tonight I feel positively *radiant*.

So I keep listening and soon enough I'm reminded of a conversation I had with my lesbian-separatist therapist over a decade ago, sometime around the mid-'80s.

"I'm okay calling myself 'gay,' but not 'lesbian,'" I had concluded midway through one of our sessions. We had been discussing labels and identities—although we didn't use terms like "label" and "identity" at that time, in that community. I tried to explain to her that "lesbian" made me uncomfortable, because it implied womanhood. "Gay" was much easier. We both felt unsure of what to do with my lack of resonance with the same word others in our circles so greatly cherished and celebrated. We left the fruit dangling from the branch, perhaps afraid to pluck it and look too closely.

Suddenly, in present-day 1998, this recollection strikes me as extremely important. I store it in the back of my mind and keep my ears open. When I finally hear the word "trans man" a few months later, it shakes me like a sonic boom.

——•——

With cautious excitement, my friend sits me down. She tells me she's changing her name to a male-sounding moniker, that she's going to start taking testosterone so she can grow facial hair, that she's planning to have something called "top surgery"—which, I learn, is another way of saying "boob removal"—and that she's going to start living as a man.

"I'd really like your support," she finishes. "You can start by referring to me with male pronouns like 'him' instead of 'her.'"

I blink in disbelief. "You, uh...You mean you can actually do all that?"

Talk about *epiphanies*. At thirty-six-fucking-years-old, I have no idea trans men exist even though I'd noticed, a thousand times before, how much more comfortable I was when I could express my boyness. My butchness. My masculinity. Especially in the bedroom. But it truly had never occurred to me that I could do something about it beyond dildos and leather jackets. Though embarrassed and frustrated by my own ignorance, I press my friend to learn more. *Facial hair?* Hell, yeah! *Deeper voice?* Oh, God, yes! *Something other than this stupid, girly name—no offense, Mom!—that I've hated forever?* Yes, please! Where do I sign?

A few short months later, my own transition begins. As testosterone flows through my veins and my maleness emerges, the years of self-loathing and self-doubt slowly wash away. It becomes clear to me now, over fourteen years later, that all of my deception, my craving for drama and my *active rejection* of healthy behavior were rooted in my gender dysphoria. I had needed some sort of control over my own destiny, and since the road to knowing myself as transsexual had not yet been revealed, my psyche had led me down other trails. The Experience shed light on this untrodden path of self-exploration, and transition became my mode of travel.

About four years into the journey, I hit an unexpected speed bump. In therapy one afternoon, I whine about yet another bad habit I know I should give up but really don't want to.

"Well," my therapist replies flatly, "maybe you should just man up."

Man up? What the fuck? I spend the rest of the session incensed. *Man up?!* I cannot believe that she—the most revered gender specialist in the Southwest—is gender stereotyping me! I leave her office in a huff. But then I catch myself and think hard for a while. And then I think about it some more. *What was she really saying?* I listen for my truth.

Over the last ten years, I've developed my own understanding. Though I'll never know if this is actually what she meant in the moment, I've personally come to see "manning up" as a maturing process. While every person of every gender goes through maturation, I believe it's a particularly unique experience for people in transition.

Because I was already a so-called adult when I started transitioning, there wasn't much time for a replay of my formative years—those defining periods of identity development throughout which most humans grow into their correct gender. And when I finally began living in my true gender twenty years late, I was initially too busy trying to pass outward inspection to get a thorough read on what was going on inside me. Nonetheless, I was expected to act like a man. I had a lot to learn about living in the world as a visible man in a very short time, whereas my cisgender peers got a few decades.

All things considered, it's relatively easy to become a guy, and even to be accepted as one—at least for someone like me, with racial and socioeconomic privilege, education, sound health, access to resources and a strong support system. I was able to transition from female-to-male in a matter of months. In contrast, it has taken me years to man up.

By seeking my truth, I've gathered that manning up is not so much about how I'm perceived by others, but how I perceive myself and manifest that self in the world. Do I become the lyin', cheatin', wife-beatin' good ol' boy my lesbian-separatist friends predicted? Or do I choose a different path? Given my history, I certainly have it in me to pull off whatever kind of man I want to be.

Manning up is about having integrity and living with intention: meaning what I say and saying what I mean. It's about the resilience and courage I've developed through the less-than-seamless process of transitioning. It's about expressing both humility and pride, admitting when I'm wrong, apologizing without shame or excuse and being gentle with myself in the process.

I haven't made every right decision: since transitioning, I've undone a couple more relationships by making poor choices. I haven't resisted every temptation to stray from my truth. I am far from perfect, and I certainly have a lot of ego tied up in my new identity. But overall I can't help feeling that I am living and breathing the vision statement that one lost soul with a painfully girly name threw out there in a desperate attempt for me to hear.

Manning up is an act of faith, both in me and the world around me. I strive to take the power and privilege that society bestows upon my manhood and use them virtuously. Now more at ease with other people than I ever could have imagined, I no longer feel the need to conflate fact and fiction in order to prop myself up.

I'm a man living my truth and it shows. At age fifty, I'm in the best physical shape of my life, I adore my career in LGBTQ advocacy and I'm over three-and-a-half years into the happiest, healthiest, most genuinely loving and mutually caring relationship either of us has experienced in our combined century on this planet. Growing pains or no, I feel extraordinarily fortunate to have a second chance at an authentic existence—authentic not only in my gender, but in my life as a whole.

ALWAYS MOVING FORWARD

Shaun LaDue

Sitting in my kindergarten classroom, I rename myself after a character I admire in a black-and-white television movie. Father Sean is a charismatic Irish priest looking after his flock of believers. I begin to realize I am queer—though I don't know the word—as my young mind is drawn to his honesty, fairness and compassion. Father Sean doesn't hurt people, especially those who are more vulnerable; he's exactly the kind of man I want to be and nothing like the unfortunate role models life has provided me with so far.

But homosexuality and queerness go unspoken in my Far North Canadian hometown. They simply do not exist. So a child like me has to learn truths about myself alone. In a "two steps forward, one step sideways" fashion, I would eventually get to a place where identifying as trans is fathomable. But long before that, I am set up to be a strange, unclassifiable guy: born First Nations, but soon adopted into a middle-class Christian, English-Canadian home at age three.

Throughout childhood, my adoptive father is blind to how my adoptive mother physically and emotionally abuses me. Eleven years of torture—constant blows and daily reminders that I am "no good" and will "never be good enough to be loved"—take their toll. I enter adulthood at age fourteen and run away on a wintry November night to live on the streets. I sneak out to stay with a friend, only to be caught by a local social worker who claims she'll help me escape the horrors of my past. I choose to follow her and, within a few days, I've left for a larger city so I can start living in a group home.

I meet youth workers there who research my background and locate my family. For the first time, I'll be introduced to my older siblings. My goal quickly becomes to make my way back to my family of origin. So one summer day I run away on a whim and ask a close friend, much older than me, to drive me to the community where my sister and brothers are already waiting to introduce me to relatives I haven't seen in fifteen years. I spend as much time with them as I can before the social workers inevitably force me to return to a tightly-controlled state institution.

Once there, I finally encounter members of my large extended family: aunts, uncles and numerous cousins. I'm introduced as "Janie's baby," my biological mother's last born before her untimely death at the hands of an assailant identified, but never investigated, by police. Everyone knows him as her on-and-off boyfriend. I'm later told that mere months after Janie's passing, he drowned, leaving behind five children to be cared for by my mother's elderly parents and a teenage aunt.

I learn of my parents' deaths in the group home, scattered among other family tales of pain. The social havoc of residential schools, welfare and alcoholism have ravaged my family and hometown, eroding First Nations cultural identities over several decades. Therefore, the social workers feel it best I live in state care, apart from my birth family and within close proximity to adults who dictate who I'm supposed to be. But they end up spending more time trying to stop me from fleeing or finding me when I manage to escape.

One social worker keeps insisting that I am smart enough to go to university and I believe her. I ignore the others who insist that I am merely fit to become a proper "young lady." I don't feel female, but don't yet publicly identify as male. Instead, I refer to myself as "androgynous"—not too in-your-face or too outrageous for any adults to look closer at me than they already do. I've learned that I can glean very few kernels of truth from so-called "experts," and wisely keep my mouth shut about being queer.

I do, however, admit that I might be a lesbian to the social workers and group home staff, which seems to momentarily calm their apprehension about my appearance. But with no other obvious gay, lesbian or trans young adults within the town's child welfare system, I sense that they are still nervously watching as my masculinity develops; I confirm this suspicion when I read through copies of my assessment reports. Each month my case worker anxiously comments on how masculine my appearance has become.

I wear boy's jeans and colorful t-shirts under button-downs each day. On occasion, I don a pair of funky red-and-black sweat pants for fun. Inspired by flashy 80's fashion, I experiment with glitter eye shadow, dragging it down my cheeks like tear drops. I shave the sides of my thick, dark hair until there are two strips of scalp showing above each ear, which I then paint blue with food coloring.

———

Unlike many kids living in the homes, I perform well in school. At age eighteen, I pull the "I feel different, I need to get out of this small town" ploy. I attend university for a year and then join the Canadian Forces. I complete basic training and start communications training, but forego graduating because of the increasing intensity of homophobic hazing in the barracks.

Slurs are tossed around freely and recruits throw "parties" in which they hold a blanket over whoever they suspect is gay and strike them with soap bars held in socks. I fear being targeted as a lesbian; being surrounded by homophobic threats is bad enough, but I'm not sure my spirit can withstand a blanketing.

My personal dread is only heightened by an unstable political climate. During my first year of service, the mayor of Oka, Québec decides to expand a golf course over a traditional Mohawk burial ground. In response, the Mohawk resist at the next town council meeting. When the Québec Provincial Police arrive to subdue the situation, a Mohawk man shoots an officer.

Soon everyone's abuzz about the "Oka Crisis," and the Mohawk barricade themselves behind roadblocks around their territory. Once the Canadian Forces are called to monitor them, I regularly endure racist comments and questions about whether I reach military standards, simply for being First Nations. It's not long before I decide it's time to leave and, after a year's service, I return home to finish my bachelor's degree in Education.

When I successfully graduate three years later, I still haven't made concrete future plans. Instead, I fly along by the seat of my pants, jumping from one possibility to the next until I find something I think might be fulfilling in the teaching field. Being in the classroom with young, eager minds prove invigorating; working at the local youth detention center, several middle schools and a local archeological dig inspires me creatively.

But after teaching for three years at the same school, I begin to feel restless and sense my career becoming thwarted by the school's administration. Though I apply to be the English and Social Studies teacher, I am stuck in the "First Nations Arts and Culture" position instead. I spiral downward into feeling unhappy, unhealthy, lost, confused and frustrated. Meanwhile, my personal life is stagnant. I marry Glenn, my college sweetheart, during my first year of teaching. Though I truly love him, our relationship only lasts as long as my first teaching stint.

I'm still like a child listening to the "adults" from my youth, the former social workers who told me that all I needed was an education, a career and a marriage to make me whole. I slowly realize that I've bought into their theories and blindly done what is expected of me, pushing aside my former dream of teaching around the world. One day, though, I've had enough. I leave my husband abruptly; I pack my bags and move into my own apartment. Soon I leave Canada entirely to spend a year teaching English in Ulsan, South Korea. When I return, my head is swirling with fretful thoughts about who exactly I am.

Am I a teacher? If so, I want to be inspiring, not just mediocre: I *need* to teach academic subjects, not just arts and crafts. Am I meant to be a writer? If so, I should find a job that gives me time to write. I should finish creating that book I started writing for entertainment as a child. Am I who I was truly meant to be at all? If not, I'm going to have to do some work to admit that I'm transgender—a new word in my adult vocabulary.

After ten years of post-college soul-searching and of healing invisible wounds from the childhood abuse I endured, I begin reintroducing myself to myself. I am curious about recurring fantasies I experience in which I have a penis, have a girlfriend and have children with her. I dream about being a regular guy—a feeling that I'm like everyone else, that I'm not letting the adults in my life down—in quiet moments throughout the day and just before going to sleep.

Now in my mid-thirties, my first step is to focus on writing and going to therapy to learn to accept that the past trauma is a part of me, but that I can also move beyond it. For another decade I move around Canada, jumping between provinces, touching down briefly in several different towns. I'm still running away, but I eventually come to realize that the only one I'm avoiding is me. It's time to face the man I was meant to be.

———

Though I spent my first post-adolescence dressing androgynously, I had incrementally shifted towards a butch lesbian style throughout adulthood. In my mid-forties, I start to dress in a way indistinguishable from any other man out there. Beginning a social and medical transition to manhood turns out not to be traumatic or even particularly shocking to those who know me well. A few of my ex-partners are even expecting it. I don't dramatically change my wardrobe; I hold onto the jeans, t-shirts, dress shirts and leather jacket I have worn since leaving the military.

I do, however, take out six of the seven rings studding my earlobes and no longer wear any jewelry besides a silver bear claw pendant hanging on a leather thong around my neck. I feel more like a man with fewer accessories. The silver pendant remains as a spiritual link to my cultural background. The grizzly bear, protector of my people, is guarding me always.

I don't change how I interact with people. I am still shy but warm up quickly, especially to women, although I'm getting used to the banter and sexual innuendo of cisgender men in my neighborhood. Since age fifteen, I've been open about how I fall in love with *people*, not what's between their legs. In the group home, my peers and social workers used to respond, "That means you're bisexual." Today, I simply laugh at the memory because I was never bisexual: I'm pansexual and still fall in love with people regardless of their genitalia, gender expression, sexual orientation or gender identity. I'm most attracted to how someone draws me in, accepts me for me and how they treat me and themselves. I have loved cisgender men and women, trans folks and genderqueer people.

A simple list of words—pansexual, trans, First Nations, poor—doesn't tell much about who I really am. There are other words that describe me better: witty, charming, intelligent, sensual, honest, caring, compassionate and loving. There are fewer preconceived notions about the person behind such descriptors, rather than those social labels. Possessing these qualities, I am not deviant or confused; I am just an ordinary person with depths of soul, of spirit, of longing.

Today, I live in the most destitute part of Vancouver: the Downtown Eastside. Those who live here are lost souls usually looking for a way out of a bleak existence and they often find it through addiction and crime. For every person who moves away or perishes, there is always someone to fill their vacated spot. I thank the Creator that I have never felt the need to escape my daily realities through these heart-breaking methods. For me, living here is just a way to bide my time until I find something better within my limited price range.

I witness how those around me have been irreversibly damaged by state-run residential schools and their lasting legacy of forced assimilation. I am one among many in the "Stolen Generation," born right after the schools closed. Like me, my "stolen" peers are First Nations children who were taken away from their families to be brought up in white homes, in hopes that they would become colorful Christians with strong work ethics. The program was doomed to be unsuccessful and, unsurprisingly, simply produced more damaged First Nations people.

When I go out for my daily walks—dressed like most of the other Downtown Eastside guys in my faded jeans, t-shirt and hoodie—I am never harassed or assaulted. I can sometimes achieve the "clean cut young man" look I actually desire through fancy clothes gathered at Christmas sales and gifted from family members. But I find that when I dress that way—in a button-down shirt, tie, jacket and leather shoes—I am immediately hounded for spare change or cigarettes.

"You look good enough to take home to mom," a homeless woman might call out to me, probing for a possible handout. While men rarely approach me, women often use their feminine charms to try to soften me up, attempting to break the ice with careful smiles and witty comments about my good looks. Their tactics don't work, but only because I don't smoke and rarely have money. Sex workers, too, eye me up and down, trying to decide whether I'm a potential trick. In return, I smile and ask, "How's it going? You okay?" without judgment. I want them to know I mean no harm.

My family of origin and I are not close in many ways because we are separated by miles, lifestyles and history. But whenever a family member comes down from the North, I make sure I'm available to meet them at the airport, take them around the city or visit the hospital if they're here for medical reasons. I only go home to the Far North about once a year to visit.

Last time I went, I came out to my whole family about starting to medically transition. They accepted my transition with the respect and grace the Kaska people are known for. However, because they do not live nearby, all they see of my physical transformation are pictures I post to Facebook. I imagine it can be a shock, but they continue to be supportive and honor my choices to stay in an urban area, transition, change my name and love who I love regardless of their sex or gender.

Knowing that they only get to practice a few weeks each year, I appreciate how hard my family tries to use male pronouns when referring to me. It doesn't bother me because I'm very comfortable in my skin now. Eventually I'll have changed physically to the point that my gender identity will not be called into question. Most importantly, *I* know I'm a man and a good one at that. Like Father Sean, who I named myself after so long ago, I am compassionate, honest, caring and willing to help those in need. I have finally figured out that living is about moving forward, always moving forward.

Souga Sin La. (Thank You)

MASCULINE VULNERABILITIES,
HUMAN CONNECTIONS

Loren Cannon

Much of my history smells like chlorine and has the oddly pleasing texture of rubber goggle straps. My whole life, swimming has given me a place to think. Perhaps, more importantly, it has given me a place to *avoid* thinking and be content to listen to the rhythm that makes up so much of the experience of the sport. The sounds of my breath, my hands entering the water and the *whoosh* as liquid moves past my skin are as percussive as they are meditative.

I had to think long and hard about the changes that would result from my social and physical transition and I worried that swimming would suffer. As it turned out, the community pool became the setting of my further education—on masculinity, on vulnerability and on how they so often come together in bodies and minds on their way to coming apart.

I had the privilege of being able to afford top surgery just three months after starting T. I got back into the water as soon as I could, but after the familiar solace of swimming a few miles in the pool, I've begun avoiding the shower after my workout. Instead, I go right to the small bathroom stall to change clothes and then quickly leave the building. This routine—disrobing in a cramped space to make sure others don't see my atypical body—is always an inconsistent end to my otherwise liberating workout experience.

For me, the locker room involves actively covering aspects of my past and the parts of my body which make that past evident; in contrast, the pool always feels like my second home. Out on the deck, I am completely comfortable walking around in just my trunks. My male-looking chest does not out me as anything but athletic. Embraced by the water, I feel both powerful and free; no one questions me, except to ask about my swimming history.

"So, are you a competitive swimmer?" asks the gray-haired man in the lane next to mine.

"I used be." I smile. At age forty-eight, I cherish what my body can still do and the joy that such movement gives me.

Yet, after the luxury of feeling so thoroughly comfortable in my own skin and physical abilities, I become a resident alien once I cross the border of the locker room. It isn't that I'm not generally accepted in this space, but I worry that this is conditional on keeping my biological history hidden. I am received well due to what I appear to be when mostly clothed: a cisgender man.

My passing privilege ends with the removal of my trunks. It is unnerving to think that others seeing my genitals could render me vulnerable to social trauma or violence and threaten my vitally important freedom of using my local pool. So I engage in strategic locker room management.

Managing my post-swim experience means I plan nearly every aspect of my time from the end of my workout to leaving the facility completely. I make sure to purchase an athletic bag with a stiff bottom panel that can balance more easily atop the toilet or hand rails along the wall. Out of the two stalls, I usually choose the handicap-accessible one for the bit of extra room it offers. As I'm in there dressing, I worry that a swimmer with a different kind of physical challenge will need the toilet.

My ritual of changing clothes in a cramped space is made easier by the fact that I am particularly small and well-balanced. It is no easy feat standing on one foot, switching to the next and removing my swim trunks to step into my boxers, all the while keeping my towel, goggles and dry clothes out of the toilet. Being larger would prevent me from changing in so small an area, and this in itself would keep me from using the pool.

I get in and out as quickly as I can; until my boxers are on I strive to be unseen, unheard and unnoticed. I am a ghost until covered, after which I can again take my place among the other men in the locker room.

———

I generally skip the shower because it would be just one more chance for others to notice I am different. But one evening I decide to quickly rinse off to avoid the usual itch of chlorine from keeping me awake at night. As I enter the open shower area, two other guys happen to follow close behind. "This is bad news," I think to myself. I feel most comfortable being alone in there.

Taking my place at the only open showerhead between the other men, I busy myself with the soap dispenser as, almost in unison, they climb out of their trunks to shower naked. This is, of course, the norm, but being right between them makes me feel how obvious it must be that I shower with my trunks on.

I wish that I, too, could shower nude, to feel comfortable enough in both the way I think others perceive me and how I perceive myself to show all of my skin. I wish that I didn't have to give a thought to my body's details and how they would inspire others to react. There is a sameness that clothed bodies enjoy. In contrast, naked bodies display both a range and generality of body parts and, as I'm told, a sense of freedom and belonging in one's skin, as well as acceptance by others.

But I fear that my body falls outside the realm of welcome diversity. So my trunks stay on and I feign nonchalance throughout my showering ritual as I stay alert to indications that I am noticed. No such signs emerge.

The shower room scene leads me to reflect on my former life as a lesbian in which penises still seemed somewhat mysterious. Now I'm quite used to them, but I'm careful to never glance directly toward a man's privates. In my experience of male spaces, at least those that are predominantly heterosexual and cisgender, checking out another's genital area is severely frowned upon. Homophobia runs deep, so looking at another man's body with any interest seems to be regarded as both sexual and unwanted. I struggle with knowing that while I find homophobia abhorrent, the practice of averted gazes benefits me personally. I don't want anyone to look too close.

After waiting out both shower mates so they don't catch on to how I avoid the open rows of lockers, I leave the shower and beeline to my little stall of safety. All the while I can't help but shake the feeling of being vulnerable, of needing to watch my back. I am not generally overly anxious, even in such a space, but my danger-antenna is on high-alert.

I change into my boxers and jeans but keep my shirt off for as long as possible. If others notice that some parts of me don't seem quite right—that I lack a bulge in my trunks, that I shower with my suit on, that I change in the stall—at least I have my male-contoured chest and facial hair to confirm that I'm in the "right" locker room.

Admittedly, all of this passing management is tedious and doesn't support my conviction that people of all body types and genital formations should be able to comfortably use the public swimming pool. Still, I'm not here for political reasons; I'm just here to swim. While I value, and at times participate in, trans activism, this does not pervade every aspect of my life.

Perhaps I remain apolitical because swimming is so precious that I fear losing it if I push too hard against the status quo. Perhaps my desire to blend in is due to the exhaustion I feel from being a very out trans man in my small local and university community. Still further, I think I long for an uncomplicated, even elegant, experience with water and movement that is insulated from the complexities and controversies that come with my identity. My goal is merely to use the facility and leave without incident.

From the stall I enter the open changing area barefoot, in jeans and shirtless. I put my bag down on a bench, preparing to dry my back and finish dressing. I glance around to confirm that the men from the shower have left.

———

I know that most of the time other guys don't notice anything about my body's condition, but I don't feel in a position to take chances. Acknowledging the potential reality of trans-directed violence comes with the territory. All of my navigation has become second nature, particularly on nights like this, when I have a gut feeling that something is going to go really sour.

Just then a man I hadn't seen before—white, with piercing blue eyes and a beard—catches my eye as he walks behind me to his locker. This form of eye contact strikes me as all wrong; in my experience, guys don't look other guys directly in the eye when in the locker room unless they know each other well. The space between me and the back wall is slim, affording a physical closeness regularly avoided unless there is no other option.

He has just broken two unspoken rules, which is reason enough to be careful. If I am being seen as not-a-real-guy, then the tenets of eye contact and space wouldn't even apply. I have seen many instances in which a man who wishes to show power over a woman will come too close and invade her space just to show that he has the social privilege to do so. I wonder if this is what is going on here.

After passing by, he locks eyes with me *again*. I try not to visibly react but am internally gauging whether my intuitions will prove correct. I can feel my heart beating faster as I attempt to appear more formidable than I really am. Then, the guy leans within an inch of my face.

"Hey, aren't you a little young to have tattoos?"

I don't know quite what to say. This isn't what I was expecting and it's a strange question to ask whether one is in a men's locker room or not.

"No. I'm older than I look," I respond in my lowest, gruffest voice.

I only briefly glance over and then coolly unzip my bag, attempting to end the conversation in a masculine, "I got shit to do" way. My back is straight, my chest is out, my stance is stable, and my attitude is annoyed indifference. I'm not looking at this guy, but down at my athletic bag—attempting to appear unapproachable and, yes, maybe even superior. I don't think of myself as better than him, but try to convey the message that I belong and am unafraid.

"Well, you don't look very old. How old are you?" he persists.

The last question makes me look a bit closer at my inquisitor. Asking a stranger's age is usually socially inappropriate in a public venue and, from my experience, particularly so in the conversational desert of the men's locker room. He doesn't seem to notice this, or that he is still standing a tad too close for comfort. I look at him and notice that his pale blue eyes stare back at me slightly unfocused. Despite being old enough for a full beard, he lacks the muscularity that one would expect from an adult man; he seems, in some ways, almost childlike.

When I respond that I am forty-eight years old, he tells me he is twenty-four: exactly half my age. I now begin to realize that he is not a threat; rather, he is probably more vulnerable than I am in many ways. Phrases doctors may use to describe him cross my mind: "mentally challenged," "developmentally disabled," or perhaps more specific diagnoses to describe his differences. He probably has been psychologically categorized by some doctor somewhere, just like I have been.

As I begin to more clearly understand the nature of the interaction, my danger-antenna leave their high-alert status and droop like cooked spaghetti. In the space of a few minutes, I go from preparing to counter my vulnerability by any means necessary—including attempts at macho coolness, tough talk and physical posturing to convey my battle-readiness—to realizing that I am in a place of influence as a tattooed older man talking to a young man interested in tattoos.

My body serves as witness to my life experiences; it presents visual clues not just to my biological, but also to my *inked* history. I realize I had been thinking unnecessarily about the former, when it was the latter that was of concern to the young man. "This guy," I think to myself, "doesn't care about the junk in my trunks—he only cares about the ink on my arms." And despite his awkward sense of conversational norms, he *really* wants to talk about it.

When I respond, I sense that he is an individual who probably isn't regularly listened to or engaged with by strangers and that I have the privilege to choose whether to heed my blue-eyed friend or ignore his attempts at connection. This privilege comes from many sources. Most obvious is my experience of being tattooed, but also as a person who has psychologically developed in a mostly typical fashion, who is able-bodied, athletically trained and educated in ways that are socially valued.

I could continue communicating in only short, terse sentences that convey exasperation and leave within a few minutes. Yet I realize that his shots at communication have left him vulnerable to my rejection, just as I am left vulnerable to rejection by others who regard my identity or body as illegitimate or even immoral. No longer feeling threatened, I wish to match his trust in me with equal trust in a person with his own point of view who strives for kinship across differences seen and unseen.

So we talk. Our conversation starts with tattoos: how they are permanent, if they hurt and how to choose a design. Eventually this leads to other topics. We talk about the types of snacks available at the pool and then discuss the new *Spiderman* movie, how the "Lizard Guy" is going to be in the sequel and how cool his lizard tail looks when trailing behind him to smash cars and buildings.

Even though I find myself wishing I could talk to him longer, the emotional whiplash of preparing myself to be a potential victim, only to realize that I am an agent of privilege, leaves me restless. I say goodbye and wish my new friend well.

———

When I reflect on this interaction, I realize how much my feelings of vulnerability, even when they seem legitimate and self-sustaining, limit my contact and fellowship with others, especially those in a position to reject or harm those aspects of myself and my world that I most value. My chest puffing and attempts at appearing self-contained, confident and masculine tell more, in this case, about my feelings of vulnerability, rather than my strength. I recall how often I have witnessed other men doing the same when, as I now suspect, they felt threatened by others' perceived privilege.

As a white, married college instructor, I possess plenty of social access to which others have responded with various forms of masculine bravado. I had once dismissed this as foolishness at best or, at worst, the evil embodiment of patriarchy itself. Now I believe that such displays are not always primarily about asserting dominance over others, but instead reflect fear—often that of being thrown out of the club of "real" men.

For many men, both trans and cis, acceptance into this fraternity is extremely fragile and being denied membership is rarely insignificant. Female acculturation and coming of age in the '70s and '80s meant the voices influencing me characterized men as typically violent and this kind of puffer-fish masculinity, so stereotypically expressed, as all there was to manhood. In some ways depictions of men have changed since my youth, but in many others they've remained much the same.

These characterizations ignored men who suffer due to lack of traditional masculinity. They failed to recognize the complex experiences within which men respond to other social pressures—and forget how these experiences vary along other vectors of privilege such as race, class, ability, sexual orientation and citizenship status. Masculinity was thought to be either dangerous or trivial, and there were no other options.

As a trans man, I have had the opportunity to reconsider gendered norms, to assess whether what I once learned about men is actually true. I've had the uncommon privilege to hear women discuss men, and men discuss women. Navigating the locker room, I often wonder if my behavior is grounded not in my personal experience as a man in this highly gendered space, but more related to stories I've heard women tell about men's inherently, predictably brutal natures.

I intimately understand the shortcomings of a sex-gender system that ties gender identity, social role, sexual orientation and even everyday clothing choices unambiguously to physiological characteristics, neatly dividing the adult human population into *men* and *women*. While I deny the significance of biology to gender or that gender identity comes in only two flavors, I also recognize that there are many out there who wish to be acknowledged and respected as men, and many others who wish to be acknowledged and respected as women.

And I now understand, through lived experience, that masculinity is more complex than a mixture of violence and superficial posturing. Instead, it can be about mutual respect, acknowledgement, responsibility and compassion.

These days I find myself, despite my history, of being in a position to acknowledge other men and model a kind of masculinity whose source is not in fear, but in quiet confidence, compassion and openness. Such an attitude, I believe, encourages connection and belonging, rather than the isolation that results from performances of indifference. Manhood, like the traditional notion of brotherhood, need not serve as a means to keep people *out*, but can be a setting within which to welcome people *in*.

I will probably always have to manage the locker room experience differently than most men, but this is only a small part of living my life. And now I know that the next time I see my new friend, I'll re-introduce myself and ask his name, prepared to spend more time chatting. I'd be pleased to look directly into his blue eyes and to see how his face lights up when we share common ground. Perhaps in the future we can be allies for each other.

THE STONE IN MY SHOE

Ezekiel Reis Burgin

I've heard that humans can't remember pain. We remember having felt it, but not the pain itself. Supposedly this is how those who give birth are willing to do it again. All that remains after the fact is the recognition that "yes, that was painful," but the visceral agony is beyond reach.

It's been exactly two years, two months and seventeen days since I went into the hospital to finally have my longed-for top surgery, but who's counting? Actually, not me. Without looking it up, going through old emails that refer to the event, I can't recall the day. I suppose I could narrow it down, but for practical purposes the actual date has slipped my mind as fully as what I ate for breakfast yesterday. It's not that surgery wasn't significant—far from it. But the *event* itself wasn't.

What do I remember? I remember that afterwards it took only a few weeks to recover. I remember that, to my surprise, I barely needed to use any painkillers. I remember that I had expected to be disgusted by the draining process but instead found it intriguing. And finally, I remember that within mere weeks I couldn't even recall what my former body had felt like.

My new body felt like it had always been mine; there was no body but this one. The form I had inhabited before was less than a memory; it was a memory of a memory, a picture in an envelope kept in a drawer, unopened for years.

I recoil at the stereotypical framing of the trans experience as being born in the "wrong" body. In so many ways, I was born into the right body—a body that can lift and bend and play piano for hours, a body that is connected on a basic genetic level to two of the people I cherish most in this world. The way I see it, there is no one "male" body for cisgender men; why then should there be a single "male" body that *I* must aspire to? I am a man, so my body—including my chest before and after surgery—is, and was, a man's body.

———

All the same, I must acknowledge that in one way I personify the "wrong body" stereotype: for me, having breasts was just *wrong*.

I know I had them. I know they hung off me and had a certain weight and heft, although I can't remember the exact feeling. I know they got in the way, were impossible to bind effectively and that I despised them. Oh yes, I remember *that* feeling.

I remember they tainted my relationship with the rest of my body, spreading like an infection so that I took no comfort in any part of me. I remember being unable to explain precisely to others this profound, inherent sense of *wrongness* that my breasts caused.

When I was a teenager and had already developed the large breasts I would carry for the next nine years, my parents brought home a book entitled *That Takes Ovaries!* for my little sister. At the time, I identified as a woman and had no conscious awareness of being genderqueer, trans or a man. When I perused the book, I was struck by a piece from a woman named Lynda Gaines about her decision to get a double mastectomy following a breast cancer diagnosis.[1] The first thing that popped into my head was *I wish I could get cancer, too.*

I *knew* that there was no way I could medically justify removing my breasts, so I became fixated for years on the idea of cancer "forcing" that necessity. Knowing that my maternal grandmother had died of the disease when I was a toddler, I found myself wondering—despite the fact that hers hadn't been breast cancer—if I could somehow inherit and direct it toward the right (that is, the oh-so-wrong) part of my body.

36

In the past I have sometimes used my teenage experience as "proof" that I was, or am, "really" trans. But the truth is, I grew up relatively content with being a girl. I relished being a protective older sibling, driving around at night with my sister, the car windows down, listening to music. I loved being a scary, hairy feminist, laughing at the girls in the changing rooms who, scandalized by my armpits, whispered, "Who does she think she is? French?!" I enjoyed setting stereotypes about "girls" on their heads by being the girl who broke the rules. Being a kick-ass girl who listened to Nina Simone, Ani DiFranco and the Indigo Girls was a cherished part of my identity back then, just as surely as being a kick-ass guy who listens to Nina Simone, Ani DiFranco and the Indigo Girls is today.

Nonetheless, my breasts were just plain *wrong*. Not because they made me "female-bodied"—they didn't. Not because I never identified as a woman—I had. Not because they were a speed bump to my being correctly gendered—testosterone would actually prove to be an essential part of the equation. No, my breasts were wrong simply because they were in and of themselves a problem: a physical embodiment of wrongness.

I can't deny the boon that surgery has been: it, along with testosterone, is the reason I'm correctly identified by others as a man about 85% of the time. Because of this, I can more easily laugh off that final 15%.

But even if people gendered me incorrectly 100% of the time, top surgery would still have been worth it. It would be worth it for when I lie down to sleep at night without my chest getting in the way. And for when I get up in the morning without the weight that had been there, unbalancing me emotionally, if not physically. For releasing me from the bras and binders that drew my attention to my chest day in and out, alone or in public. For allowing my cats to settle on top of my Buddha belly rather than jumping awkwardly onto a shelf beneath my chin.

I'm not saying that I've become a Zen master (belly notwithstanding). Surgery was not a magic wand, and I don't walk around in a golden haze of blessed joy and peace. When a cashier says, "Have a good day, ma'am," it still brings me up short in frustration. But where before each "ma'am" or "ladies" used to feel like the speaker had casually reached up through my stomach to rip out my heart and nonchalantly drop it in the dirt, now it is no more than a prick.

Once, my life was made up of moment after moment of being reminded of my chest; these days it is not. These days I don't have to think of any of this, except as I write this chapter and explain myself. *That* is the reason I had surgery. I go to work, to the grocery store, to friends' houses, to the beach and I finally don't have to think about my body. People tend not to notice what's going right, or—to put it a better way—what's not going wrong; they don't constantly think about their *not* itching skin, their *lack* of hunger or the fact that they *don't* have a pebble underfoot.

Before surgery, I was walking around with a sharp stone in my shoe, and there was no way I could ignore it. Now? I walk unencumbered.

———

I've never been terribly good at keeping secrets. Within three months of coming out to myself as trans*, virtually everyone in my life knew as well. Ironically enough, one of the first people I told was a friend I gossiped with during lectures in our psychology class. He immediately looked at me with shock: *he* had been moments away from coming out to *me* as trans. This is the kind of environment that I have mostly lived in ever since: surrounded by a community of other trans* men.

Hindsight is more than 20/20: it seeks patterns, trying to make sense of the past in the context of the present. In terms of my gender identity, this is undeniable. The temptation emerges especially when cis folks try to find out "how long" I've been trans. They rarely like my answers, which fail to conform to what they think trans-ness "should be." They want to pin it firmly in the past, as an inherent "born like this" or perhaps an "I've always known" instead of the more elusive, but honest, choice/not-choice that I experienced. My story—and most people's stories, I believe—isn't quite so clear-cut.

I said earlier that I was fairly happy being a girl throughout my teenage years. Yet this isn't entirely accurate: I didn't like pink. Not because of any intrinsic qualities but because of its social meanings: feminine, girly, weak—in a word, *lesser*. I felt the same about shopping, skirts and makeup. Like many young girls and women, I believed that liking "girly things" would make me less hip, less interesting, less capable, even while I denied the existence of inherently "girly things." I bought into the lie that girls who are feminine are "catty" or "fake," even while castigating male friends for their more overt sexist assumptions and jokes as to what individual women could be or do.

I definitely identified as a feminist, but it was a sort of Second Wave feminism that held that being butch is better than being femme, that carpentry is a loftier aspiration than childcare, that being "tough" is better than being "weak"—all while insisting that women and men are equal. In short, like many girls before me, I had internalized our society's sexist, femme-phobic attitudes; I had decided that in order to "rise above" sexism, I needed to shun anything culturally associated with femininity. In this way, I *was* a typical girl.

———

Amusingly, some of my first inklings that I was trans arose from realizing that I wasn't butch. I wanted to be seen as masculine, but I don't walk, talk or emote in the "right" ways to be butch. I scare easily enough, I like to laugh and, yes, be girly; I like to bake and squeal over cute animals and I've always been better at the more sinuous, femme-style dance moves than those more solid, slow and stationary butch ones.

"Why can't you just be a butch lesbian?" my mother asked me when I came out to her. "Because I'm not butch and I'm not a lesbian," I told her. Recognizing my gender has meant allowing my femininity to reemerge. I see now that I can be *both* "masculine"—because I am a man—and "feminine" in my behaviors and actions without needing to shoehorn myself into an identity that doesn't quite fit.

So the picture of me as a reasonably happy girl is thus both true and untrue. But along with that ambiguous picture I recall little moments that seem to point more clearly to the transgender man I have become.

At the time I didn't connect each of the moments with anything larger, but at college they coalesced into a more coherent picture.

My maternal grandfather has three daughters and each of these daughters has two children. My mother's sisters each had a boy first, then a girl. As a child, I decided I was one of my family's "boy cousins" since I was the older child. (A recent observation: all of the "girl cousins" in my family started to get gray hairs in their late teens; the boys did not. I do not have a single gray hair.)

Playing pretend as a preteen, I'd imagine myself as video game hero Sonic the Hedgehog, rescuing the girl. In middle school, while pondering a new middle name—as, with my parents' consent, I was moving forward with a legal change—I decided on "Gabriel." "No daughter of mine is going to have a boy's name for a middle name!" was my father's response.

As a teenager I spent years consuming media about trans women and men, and even got into an argument with an adult during one Thanksgiving dinner regarding the legitimacy of trans* identities. It might seem obvious from this alone that I would recognize myself as trans one day.

Yet, many of these moments can be construed in other ways. Deciding that I was a "boy cousin"? A logical deduction for a seven year old seeing a pattern and wanting to fit himself into it.

Playing make-believe as a boy? Our society teaches girls that boys get all the fun adventures.

Arguing with a family friend? I grew up in a family that prized social justice and was simply standing up for those who had no voice.

When cis people ask me "how long" I've been trans, I sense they want a story that includes all of these background elements: they want me to say that I was "born this way," or that I knew since I was seven because I thought of myself as a "boy cousin," or perhaps that I knew since age ten because I played pretend as a male hero. But the truth is, I consider my journey to knowing myself as trans as starting when I arrived at my all-women's college. Even though I'd been reading stories with trans* characters for years, it took seeing real live trans* men for me to start thinking about myself as potentially a man as well.

———

My first year in college was one of confusion. Many of the trans* guys and genderqueer folks I saw were very slender. Their slim bodies made it easier for them to be perceived as men, or at least be considered androgynous; they didn't have round faces or curvy hips like me. I found myself drawn to them but was unsure whether it was their gender identities or just their skinny bodies that I envied.

By the end of the year I concluded that I was actually coming face-to-face with my own internalized fat-hatred. Nevertheless, over the next two years I found myself participating primarily in campus groups and communities that had trans* members.

After that, I can't say for sure what happened. Some of it was knowing more and more guys who were fat or chubby like me, seeing that it was possible to be trans without being some willowy, tall, angular guy. Some of it was working on my own shame about my fatness and realizing that I still envied the guys on campus. Some of it was coming to terms with the fact that though I wanted desperately to be perceived as butch, my friends were telling me that I just plain *wasn't*.

What I do know is when this particular journey ended: midway through my junior year I became intensely focused on renaming myself Ezekiel. I didn't know precisely why, but the name just suddenly felt right, and my old name suddenly felt wrong.

This didn't particularly shock me; I'd changed my name before when I was ten (though it was another year or two before my parents made it legal). A second name change at twenty seemed in keeping with the pattern. (I joke that when I turn thirty-three we'll know if the pattern is holding.)

After a few weeks of mulling over a name change, I realized that a pronoun change to go with it would be just right. Which brings me back to that psychology class, the week or so after spring break, when I told my friend that I was changing my name and going by "he" just as he was about to tell me the very same thing.

So, is my narrative trans "enough"? I don't really care. I *am* trans* and this *was* my childhood and my journey.

I think there are more of us out there than cis society—or trans* communities, for that matter—wants to imagine. More of us who somehow chose to be trans* or who grew up to become trans* without having had a straightforward childhood of "wrongness." More of us who can feel strongly about our gender and how we are perceived while also holding on lovingly to aspects of our gendered pasts.

———

After I came out, but before surgery or hormones, my sense of community was tied quite firmly to this transgender identity of mine. I restarted trans* organizations on campus, educated peers and professors in class, excitedly went to see other trans* academics and worked with local trans* activists. My friend groups, too, were overwhelmingly trans-masculine.

Within these communities, we created a world where our lives were the norm instead of the outlier. Where it was unremarkable, even common, to talk about binders or top surgery, pronouns and name changes. Where people understood the trans* meaning of words and where certain things didn't need to be spoken of because we all already knew.

But these days I've started to realize that I have been welcomed more readily into cisgender society since I had surgery and started hormones. I no longer need to seek out other trans* and genderqueer men in order to be considered "normal"—at least if I don't mention my trans status. I am no longer as aware, moment to moment, of whether I am being perceived as a man or as a woman, because the perception skews ever more towards my truth. I've even had cis gay men include me in their "we" when telling the cultural stories people tell and that has been a heady experience for me—a fat trans* man who worried I would never be accepted by this other community of mine.

Yet something has been missing in these moments.

Who is my community now? Who do I seek out, who do I strengthen and draw strength from in return? I go back to where I started, and then expand it. My community is my trans* brothers, but it is also the trans* women of color who are rarely the face of "our" movement but who are the most targeted amongst us; it is my fat mentors and those other writers and luminaries with disabilities who are routinely desexualized by a society that can't see "how" "they" would "do it"; it is the cis men and women of color of my city who are hyper-sexualized daily because brown bodies have always been considered public property; it is my friends who are poor or working class or houseless—or all of the above—who are rarely even treated as if they were *people*, let alone men or women; it is genderqueer boys and girls (and bois and grrls), sex workers of all genders and sexualities and anyone else who is Othered, excluded or marginalized.

And if I no longer share their (our?) daily pain because my chest is how I like it, because I don't get cat-called on the street anymore and because I pause for only a second before going into the men's room instead of waiting all day as I used to? Then I respectfully ask that they let me be their sidekick, their ally and promise I will try to remind myself every day where I came from and not forget that, while I don't have that stone in my shoe any longer, I still remember how it hurts.

DIMENSION Z

Rayees Shah

The third dimension or dimension Z—that most familiar of planes where I have twirled through much of life—dimension Z: that's what I want to talk about. In a linear world comfortable with the notion of existing on an XY plane, my tangential existence on the Z plane has been a source of much confusion, dismay and fear that, fortunately for me, has been balanced by wonderful understanding, true love and undying loyalties.

My focus here will be the identities: the faith, gender and sociocultural ones that I continuously struggle to knit together in a seamless pattern. My faith identity is the constant X variable that has been the fulcrum around which the Y variable of my sociocultural identity and the Z variable of my gender identity have been pivoting. I chose this XYZ paradigm because it most closely resembles my yearning to understand the mysteries of physics, or physical life, in parallel to understanding the mysteries of ultimate reality, or spiritual life.

My earliest memories are of my mother reminding me to speak like a girl; when I first started to talk, I somehow preferred to speak in the male gender since Urdu, my native language, is gender-specific. By the time I was seven I had learnt three important lessons. In no particular order, I learnt that I was different because I knew with an innate certainty that I was a boy yet could not persuade those around me to recognize this reality and instead suffered punishing consequences when I tried.

I tried everything from earnest, childish arguments that I could never strengthen with proof to grand tantrums when I rebelled against wearing frilly frocks. Nothing worked. Eventually, I simply evolved into a tomboy; I gave up the arguments and the attempts at reasoning. I remained a girl and acted at every opportunity like a boy.

In the meantime, I discovered that my spirit flew into joyous ecstasy whenever I was outdoors. I somehow understood that the muddy pools after summer rains, the smell of freshly mowed grass on the golf course and the singing nightingales heralding the mango season was where God was to be found.

Somehow the brimstone and hellfire teachings that were crammed upon me from different elders never really scared me into submission. It was beyond belief that the God of Nature—the maker of bird songs and beckoning trees—could be such a hard taskmaster. Yet, I again turned to pretense and mindlessly memorized the requisite verses of the Koran with no real understandings of what the ancient interpretations meant.

Finally, I learnt to be my own best friend. Girls disdainfully excluded me from their play, daunted by my hyperactive, riotous nature. Boys avoided me, fearful of my angry strength; I was known for beating up those twice my size for refusing to let me play soccer with them.

———

I became familiar with the vanities of the female ego and the delicate pride of the male one all too soon. Interestingly the servant's children—the cook, the driver, the cleaner, the gardener—did not enjoy this luxury of the ego. I soon discovered a ubiquitous truth: the servant's kids would always be willing to include me in their daily chores and to play whatever games I taught them with gusto.

Of course my mother would try to curtail my hobnobbing as best she could, but the exposure was enough to taint my perspective of my own privileged, elite status forever. Social self-reliance was probably the foundation of my later disregard for convention and my abhorrence of that fundamental fear: *What will people think?* In other words, my baby steps were taken with these lessons into dimension Z, quantum leaps away from the XY planes.

This eclectic onslaught of realizations took place against a backdrop of constant travel. I was a military brat who got to travel the length and breadth of the country whenever dad was transferred. Schools changed, friends—or the not-so-friendly brats—changed, a constant I adjusted to easily given my complete disregard for "relationship building."

By the time I started fourth grade, I had learnt to speak Urdu with a Punjabi accent, English with an Urdu accent and Punjabi like a native. Yet wherever I went, I was first and foremost a *mohajir*, an immigrant, while all the other kids in the military schools were children of the "sons of the soil": Punjabis, Pathans, Baluchis and some Sindhis from the four provinces of Pakistan and part of the pre-partition landscape of India.

The intersections of my multidimensional existence became ever more complicated. The Z of my gender identity clashed with the XY linear world of male/female, the Z of my immigrant identity collided with the XY world of native/immigrant, my multilingual skills and ability to relate to the poor sat incongruously alongside the XY planes of an elite private Catholic convent where English was the only official school language.

Over the next eight years, my personality was tamed and groomed by the Sisters of the Convent. My "wild spirit" was channeled "appropriately" into games and athletics and I became the school's star athlete, winning inter-school championships year after year. My wrath at the injustice of poverty, the imbalance between rich and poor, found powerful release in debates and dramas while my "bohemian" dress code was suitably dealt with.

In sixth grade I cajoled my mother into bringing me a pair of Western boots from one of my parents' various foreign trips. I wore my favorite denim jacket and new boots to school on my birthday: the one day a student was allowed to be out of uniform. All went well with my friends amused at my ecstasy over my new boots. They loyally tried to be excited even though their confusion was more than obvious: *Why is she so excited over a pair of boots instead of nice, pointy-heeled, patent leather shoes?*

Just my luck that the headmistress of the middle school decided to take a random tour of the classrooms that day. As Games Captain, I had the privilege of sitting in the front row, which meant Sister Mary was treated to the abomination that was "get up" in all its glory the moment she swept into the room. She was not one given to extravagant displays of emotion, so that one sharply lifted eyebrow provided a swift assessment of the extent of her disapproval. Calmly, she informed me I was to remain within the confines of the classroom for the rest of the day including recess, and leave only to go straight home. She didn't want a little boy running around in the all girls' school grounds.

This became a defining theme for much of my later life. Blessedly, I looked like a boy if I dressed like one—and I exploited this advantage to its full extent as I grew up. Meanwhile, faith, as a pillar of my identity, remained an innocent bystander while my personality evolved. By the time I graduated from high school, it had become a token tradition of mindlessly performing a ritual now and then to conform to familial religious traditions. I had begun to resent this God of my childhood: this God of beauty who punished me for unknown sins by condemning me to the pain and misery of female puberty. I had trusted Him to make me a man, but instead was trapped and betrayed by my body.

———

Relationships for a conflict-ridden creature like me were a complicated affair. However, by age sixteen—which was anything but sweet—I had managed to be in a long-term relationship with my one and only girlfriend. She had come to understand my gender crises and we had promised to marry the moment I figured out how to get myself fixed.

My relationship with my sister also underwent an amazing transformation: from arch-nemeses, we had become bosom beaux. So it was to her I first took this gender quandary. She didn't seem particularly surprised and instead reassured me that I wasn't eternally trapped since she had recently read an article in Mom's *Woman's Own* magazine about Renee Richards, a tennis player who had become a woman. So we both decided the best course of action would be to talk to Mom who, to my complete surprise, was outraged.

I was forbidden from meeting my girlfriend at whose unsuspecting door was laid all the evil in my head. My gender identity was never discussed again. Mom focused all of her energies on exhortations of prayer and forgiveness and ensuring I did my share of household chores as, until that point, my sister had happily picked up the slack I was all too willing to offer. And she, ever graceful, elegant and charming, was subtly introduced to eligible bachelors at family gatherings. She served tea on trolleys to friends of my elder brothers—even as she was vigilantly chaperoned by those same brothers.

Ours was truly a family in no man's land. Liberal, educated, independent women—anomalies in a patriarchal, conservative Islamic society where women were, by and large, uneducated, living under a veil of ignorance, subjected to patriarchal hegemony as third-rate citizens of a third world country. The women in my family existed in a bubble: we were part of the upper echelons of society, enjoying the privileges of freedom of thought and movement that left conservatives aghast and the thinking, conscience-stricken liberals disgusted at the inherent hypocrisy of it all. This was the formative world of my dimension Z.

My next few years, however surreal, were defined by radical upheavals and wrenching pain. When I was eighteen, my mother passed away after a short three-month battle with leukemia. My father was left clueless and floundering with two single daughters. My brothers were both married by then but my sister and I were still finishing our education and marriage was not at the top of our agendas.

A few months after my mother's death, my sister and I accompanied my father on our first pilgrimage to Mecca to perform "Umrah." An abbreviated version of the annual pilgrimage of Hajj, the Umrah can be performed year-round and as many times as one might wish; the Hajj, however, is mandatory at least once in a lifetime for every Muslim. By this time my relationship with God, perfunctory and tenuous at the best of times, barely existed. Yet, I hoped this pilgrimage would bring some meaning to my life. The inner peace I sought so fervently was nowhere to be found.

But the Umrah did nothing to fill the emptiness that constantly haunted my soul and consumed every fiber of my being with sorrow unlike any I had ever experienced. Suffocating under the veil wasn't conducive to fervent prayer, either. I returned from the pilgrimage and shortly thereafter moved to the city of Lahore to study architecture. I lost myself in the bohemian artistic environment. My soul submerged, I swam blithely in the murky waters of unconventional, creative thinking; I experimented with atheist philosophies and quoted poetry through the night.

My checkered educational background spring boarded from then on. I did stints in mechanical engineering, received a bachelor's in liberal arts and then an MBA in management. I traveled through East Asia, England and Europe, eventually arriving in the United States. Once there, my world changed again.

It began when I had the good fortune to befriend a trans woman online who opened the door of a hitherto unknown transgender community. This community soon became my adopted family of fellow trans men who shared my own experiences of alienation and solitude. The rich diversity of my new family astounded me with trans men and women hailing from every faith, every continent.

My friendship with a Presbyterian minister enabled me to finally reconcile my gender identity with my faith. I rekindled that long extinguished flame by once again having conversations with God. Her counseling helped me make sense of dichotomies between my faith, my social upbringing and my gender in ways I had never imagined possible. It was a journey filled with pain and sadness leavened with the silver lining of self-fulfillment.

I have found my faith again through mysticism. The acceptance of my transgender identity by my Sufi order's leader was a revelation in and of itself. Ironically, a lifelong struggle with multiple identities has brought me to a path of Sufism defined by the ideal of an identity-less existence. This is the mystic's world of oneness with Allah whereby one loses all sense of oneself as separate or distinct from the ultimate reality and systemically works to annihilate all manifestations of identity, be they religious, cultural, racial or social. There are no hierarchies of power, no regard for the matriarchal or patriarchal politics of religion. The only requirement is to strive to love, to know that love is the only ultimate truth.

———

The three dimensions of my life have developed exponentially over the last ten years. My dad's acceptance of my gender transition was a supreme irony: I had not imagined a military man taking my revelation lightly. Albeit reluctantly, he embraced me for who I am, thereby ensuring the rest of my family would come to accept me as well. My father's word was supreme law as far as my extended family was concerned, but it was reconciliation too far for my brothers. It has been fifteen long years since I have spoken to either of them.

After completing my gender transition, the exhilaration of freedom catapulted me into the world of transgender activism. I became the poster boy for the successfully transitioned female-to-male: one who managed to win the acceptance of his family and his faith community while being blessed with good health through the myriad physical changes, holding a regular job, and co-founding and leading a non-profit organization for gender education.

I then danced my way, yet again, across the increasingly intersecting planes of my multiple identities, this time in reverse gear. Not being out at work, yet attending speaking engagements and conferences nationwide for transgender education and rights, was an exercise in balancing the reality of society's fear of the unknown, the responsibility of sustaining my own livelihood and striving to realize my deepest faith foundation of translating divine love into ordinary human experience.

True to form, God continues to have a sense of humor. Reconnecting with Allah outside the boundaries of Islam's strict ritualism was not the extent of it. At a very unconventional meeting of kindred spirits, gathered to chant in remembrance of Allah, I met my wife-to-be. Her acceptance of my proposal after understanding my life history was another miracle I had only prayed for, and a whirlwind courtship was followed by a literally overnight wedding. I had overcome the challenges of many relationships from daughter to son, from sister to brother, from niece to nephew, from aunt to uncle, but nothing prepared me to be a husband.

Marital life is another twisting path I now walk, balancing the three planes of my ever-evolving identities, yet seamlessly merging into unity. True to form, my wife and I defy many of society's norms and our partnership symbolizes the best and the worst of the Odd Couple. I struggle as I write this piece to describe our relationship—so far from the ideal I had aspired to yet, in many ways, so far exceeding any ideal I could have hoped for. The nomad traveler paired with the settler, the passionate idealist in a three-legged race with the quiet stoic.

My wife is the quintessential homebody with a deeply ingrained Eastern traditional etiquette and even more deeply ingrained conservative Islamic values. She has defined my life with quiet, predictable stability even as we have come to loggerheads with my yanking her around on adventurous travels far beyond her regimented world, introducing her to social circles of eclectic LGBT gatherings and debating endlessly on the virtues of mysticism versus conventional religion. I am amazed by the depth of her compassion and the gentle tenderness of her ministrations to the sick.

Almost ten years of married life have taught me lessons in levels of acceptance and shades of understanding like nothing in my years of activism did. We all want unconditional love, the kind that loves without understanding—or, rather, without needing to understand. I am richly blessed beyond my deserving to have experienced such love from my wife. She continues to be the wind beneath my wings as we sometimes soar and sometimes just glide on low winds through life's winding ways.

———

I'll conclude this journey through time and space with a brief description of our most transforming journey: the pilgrimage of Hajj. The grueling rituals performed with millions of fellow pilgrims, the collective prayers or gratitude at the Kaaba and the crescendo of cries beseeching forgiveness in the desert plain of Arafat was an unforgettable experience, or personal witness, to the inexplicable divinity that permeates this world of ours with signs replete for those who understand.

As I stood shoulder to shoulder with my wife in the magnificent courtyard of the Prophet Mohammad's mosque in Medina, quietly chanting prayers in the twilight, I thought about the last pilgrimage I had made. I had never imagined almost twenty years ago that I would perform Hajj as a man amongst men, much less with my wife by my side. Glory be to Allah for the daily miracles that unfold so seamlessly in our lives.

I looked around me and saw people from every corner of the world all drawn together with the same yearning to realize their faith's mission of seeking closeness to the ultimate reality. But we don't have to travel around the world to find this closeness: it's in our hearts all of the time and we experience it so richly when we open our arms in loving embrace to all those different from our own selves. For in recognizing that difference, we see that one familiar light shining through eyes that no longer belong to strangers.

So silence the naysayers with peace, respect their linear XY worlds and then fling yourself with a leap of faith into dimension Z!

TRANSBOYHOOD

C.T. Whitley

I wake up early, lift my clothes from a crumpled pile on the floor and grasp a pair of pink corduroys. The knees are stained green from a few too many tackle football romps, while paint and classroom glue cover the thighs. Dirt clings to the seams, caked in the fringes of rips that collide with my trusty black kappa shoes. I grab a gray army shirt, selectively swiped from my older brother, to drape over my lean body. My hair dangles past my shoulders. Although I've always wanted to have it cut short, my mother is in love with my long, wavy blond tangles—and it is always tangled. I run downstairs to find my dad preparing to shave in his drab yellow bathroom.

"Want some on your face?" he asks, eyeing me in the doorway.

"Sure thing!" I give my usual response to our ritual. We meet daily in the basement to shave. He gently grabs the side of my face and tilts it slightly, smearing shaving cream from ear to ear.

"Yep, that looks about right," he announces amidst small talk about my adventure plans for the day. He uses the backside of his razor to glide over my soft, hairless skin, rinsing the blade in the sink after each swipe.

"I'll be working on the truck tonight. I sure could use a helper." His eyebrows lift in my direction as he finishes my face.

"I'm there!" I adore the time we spend working on his truck. With the country music cranked up, my father will call out for tools and I'll grab whatever he needs. He'll show me how each instrument works, positioning his hands over mine to demonstrate the precise movements.

"Wait, what about the smelly face stuff?"

"Aftershave? Right. I forgot the aftershave." Shaking the balm into his hands, he applies it to his face and then to mine. Now I'm ready to start my day.

This is a momentous morning for a seven-year-old. At noon, all of the neighborhood boys are meeting to ride bikes over dirt mounds in the open space at the outskirts of our rural hometown. I push my hair from my face and grab the handles of my bike. The cool wind feels good against my moist cheeks as I ride down under clear summer skies.

I show up to a parade of school-aged boys with bikes in tow. An audience of girls watches, giggling and pointing excitedly in our direction. I look over, grin and wave at the ones I know. In fact, I have a secret a girlfriend among them. We've been pretending that I'm really a boy named Alex. Whenever she comes over to play or hang out in the garage to watch my dad fiddle with his car, I am her boyfriend.

Today I feel tough, ready to ride in front of an audience, a member of the boys' club in my neighborhood. There really is no doubt: I am not like the girls adorned in frilly, pastel dresses peering from the sidelines. I am a daredevil, just one of the guys.

As I get closer to the dirt mounds, I catch the eye of a few boys I don't recognize. One gestures in my direction, subtly lifting his head to alert my friend Tim. In response, Tim stops riding to walk his bike over to me.

"Umm," he hesitates. I am unclear about what he might have to say, but can sense his discomfort. "Well. . . see, some of the other boys don't want to play with girls today."

"Sure," I reply glibly. "I think they are all watching. So let's ride." I'm imagining everyone's amazed looks when I show them my well-practiced landing.

"No, the other boys only want to ride with boys. No girls allowed. Maybe we can ride together tomorrow." He pauses, stumbling over the sadness he sees in my eyes. "Sorry," he mutters before turning to trudge off.

I kick the ground, sending up a puff of red clay that flies away in the wind, leaving behind a crimson scuff. I don't dare look in the direction of the girls as I fight back tears. Head down, I can hear the sound of tires landing hard against the mounds a few yards behind me. Tim's voice echoes through the clearing as he cheers.

———

Before that day in 1988, I was sure of my place in the male world. Then, almost overnight, boy and girl dynamics start to shift, becoming more exclusive. I am left on the perimeter, observing as the two worlds pull apart, excluded from both.

Where I was once selected as the first girl for every recess team, by nine-years-old I become the last one picked. Choices are no longer about skill—because hands down I am the most athletic person in the group—but more about fitting the roles we are expected to perform. Being left out soon escalates into active questioning from friends and strangers.

"You are *not* a boy!" "Can't you try to look like a girl?" "That's not something a girl should do." "You take the tomboy thing way too far!"

From early childhood to my late teens, I admiringly peer into the world I've been pushed out of, a boyhood lost. In the early years, I watch enviously as the boys of my small Western community become Cub Scouts. They learn knot-tying techniques and survival skills while camping in the woods. I spend months begging my parents to let me be a Girl Scout, my closest option.

The first day, I stand at attention next to my mother, framed by the doorway of our local church. I eagerly write my name on the entrance card provided and take in the decorated name tags surrounding me.

"Welcome to Daisy Scouts!" the woman behind the table exclaims, handing me a packet with "Daisy Scout" written on the cover. Turning to my mom, she continues.

"Your daughter will be presented with her uniform during the recognition ceremony next month!"

Hearing the word "uniform," I think of my friend Tim's sturdy, badge-covered attire and wonder if mine will be similar. But as the woman pulls out my new gear, I instantly balk.

I'm not against aprons *per se*; I have a small one, same as my grandfather, sitting at my grandparents' house. I'm used to it hanging about my waist whenever we make our hand-rolled noodles, its two front pockets holding all my cooking utensils. It's nothing like the blue, body-length one the troop leader now holds. I don't want it, particularly because it will cover my entire front. I can't fathom the practicality of wearing a full apron, especially into the wilderness.

When our troop goes camping in June, I see my worries are for naught: there *is* no wilderness. We have to forego tents and campfires for the shelter of a cabin or facility. Despite my disappointment at this lack of adventure, I remain a Girl Scout for several years; it's my only choice.

By middle school I finally reach my limit. I tentatively approach my mother about leaving my troop and, unfazed, she agrees that they don't seem to be the right fit for me. We decide together that we'll spend more time at our family's rustic cabin.

Nearly every weekend that summer we head to the mountains— my dream destination, though not the way I'd dreamt of getting there. Nonetheless, I rejoice by bringing friends as often as possible. We camp outside next to the cabin in our own rough shelters made of downed aspens and bed sheets, gazing up at the vast Colorado sky.

———

"Has your daughter always been like that?" I overhear a distant cousin ask at a family gathering. As I've grown, I've watched what used to be subtle questioning of my masculinity turn into blatant condemnation of my mother for allowing such deviation. Family and friends interrogate her parenting, often right in front of my face. It stings, but I'm well-versed in defending my boyish ways. Still, I worry about my mother, a gentle woman who has always been so protective of me.

Another week, an older woman approaches my mother at the grocery store.

"Your daughter is such a pretty girl. If you just combed and curled that hair and put girl's clothing on her, she would really be beautiful." I feel like a paper doll, a cardboard cutout to dress and play with. My mother nods, smiling uncomfortably.

"Thanks."

"I wish I had long, naturally-blond hair," the woman continues, undeterred. "I've been dying mine for years and I could never let it grow too long."

For the next few minutes she recommends clothing and makeup to heighten my "natural beauty" while my mom attempts to change the subject by remarking on the weather.

Not long afterwards, we hear from a family friend we run into on the street.

"Why would you let her wear that baggy shirt?" The comment cuts deep; I can see it in my mother's face though she tries not to look towards me. As usual, she makes light of the situation.

"Oh, you know how kids are. They have their own ideas of what to wear." There is something about her joking that also wounds me. Although she nominally supports my self-expression, I can't help but feel like a disappointment. In private that night, she reminds me why.

"Can you just wear a dress next week for picture day at school?"

"Sure," I say softly, trying not to take it personally. I don't want to hurt my mother any more than I already have.

"I don't want you to get teased," she explains.

"What other people say doesn't bother me," I reply untruthfully.

"Maybe what *my* friends say doesn't matter, but what about the kids at school?" she questions. We both know there's not a day that goes by that a classmate doesn't make a gender-related dig at me.

I simply sigh and, with mixed emotions, agree again to don a dress for my school picture. In this way, I can become my mother's protector, knowing full well that only such armor will fend off public disapproval. As a final statement of love and to minimize taunting at school, I also keep my hair long.

By high school, my heroics turn against me. Whereas prepubescent boys once saw me as an equal, after puberty I become a sex symbol to unfamiliar men. As I walk briskly down Main Street to my fast-food job, a chorus of them honk and shout, undaunted by my oversized uniform and tightly bound hair.

"Hey baby, I wouldn't mind seeing you in less clothing," one leers out of a sunny yellow Pontiac. I pull my shoulders forward and hunch down further. Instantly I feel dirty, betrayed by my body's curves.

"I wouldn't mind giving you a *ride*," yells another, following up with a loud whistle. I try to ignore their hollers and catcalls. I've learned at this point that countering only ensures more unwanted attention. Home is my only refuge from how battered I feel in public spaces. It begins to sink in that if this is how life is going to be, I'm not sure I can continue.

———

One fateful October morning I walk into my high school. Within minutes I feel a large, familiar hand pull at my shoulder. It belongs to a jeering football player who's just snagged my backpack before I can break free.

I watch as the bag's contents are callously tossed down the hall. I don't say a word and, as I cautiously walk over to retrieve my things, a second player comes over to kick my water bottle. It smacks against the wall and begins to leak. I notice a teacher observing in her doorway a few yards down; I look at her pleadingly, to no avail.

Spotting her as well, the boy who kicked my water bottle stops and turns back to me. "Yo, sorry!" he calls out casually before sauntering away, not bothering to help gather my belongings. The teacher turns, too, and steps wordlessly back into her classroom. This is turning out to be a typical morning.

It's followed by a typical lunch. My small group of friends and I sit in our usual ditch outside, foregoing the cafeteria for fear of being taunted. We've been eating in the same spot together for nearly four years.

The daily harassment has steadily worsened since the beginning of the school year, following an eventful picture day. A dozen of my friends and I had staged a protest by sitting front-and-center for the yearly all-school photo. We knew our location was usually reserved for popular kids and athletes, but we remained rooted there from the time school started until the picture was taken.

Strolling into the gym, several football players had noticed us and snickered at our presence. They had crossed the room and two immediately begun to yank at my legs; two others tried to rip my fingers from the bench. Quickly, a couple of administrators had approached, quietly suggesting we move to the side or top of the frame. We refused: we had just as much right to be there as anyone else. So they retreated, huddling at the center of the gym to discuss the situation, ignoring the escalating verbal and physical attacks behind them.

Eventually, the barrage stopped and the picture was taken. Curiously, though, it was not included in the yearbook nor framed and proudly hung in the main office, unlike every year before. I heard the message loud and clear. We were the visibly undesirable, a group—as we were commonly referred to by peers—of "freaks," "geeks," "gays" and "goths." I knew my decision to participate in the protest was bound to cause me harm, but it seemed worth it somehow.

It seems pointless now. I gather everything from my locker after being stripped of my backpack once again this morning. I make a decision to never return. I leave the building and drive home, deliberately looking at the trees and sky. *These will be the last images I take with me when I close my eyes.* I'm awake, but everything seems blurry. I lose track of time and soon I'm sinking into darkness.

But before the breath can leave my body completely, I'm being hauled into an ambulance and rushed to the emergency room. I feel disgusted and embarrassed. I can't even die without being hassled. Half-heartedly listening to the muddled words of the paramedics, I'm still praying that God takes me, wondering how he can be so cruel.

When I arrive at the hospital, the emergency nurses treat me as if I'm a drug addict; to them I'm just another teenage delinquent. Their maltreatment reaffirms how I feel: I am not worth saving. Somewhere, I can hear my mother weeping, devastated and hysterical. I retreat into myself then, blocking out the experience by keeping my eyes tightly shut.

"She doesn't show many of the common signs for suicide attempts," a doctor and therapist remark between themselves as I sit across from them in an office the next day. I'd been listlessly transferred to their mental health ward when I finally reached a stable condition the night before.

We discuss how I've maintained stellar grades and a job, haven't used alcohol or drugs and don't seem depressed. When I finally divulge stories of the daily torture I've endured, the therapist seems taken aback. I choose, though, to not reveal how I've felt like a boy since I was a child. I doubt she'll understand. Already humiliated by my unsuccessful suicide attempt, I remain reticent.

Despite the doctors' concern, all I can think about is escaping the ward so I can make sure to end my life. While I bide my time, the nurses treat me kindly and friends and family members visit frequently, bringing home-cooked meals. Gradually, I begin to enjoy the isolation the ward provides. Large metal doors block out the world for the week I'm under observation.

Meanwhile, my mother struggles emotionally, believing my suicide attempt was a failure on her part. Although I repeatedly assure her that it was not, I feel dreadful that I've hurt her so deeply. Knowing how much I mean to her, as well as the rest of my family and my friends, I forego ending my life, at least until I've completed college.

Secretly, I decide that during my freshman year I will explore my sexuality and gender identity and seek out campus resource centers. Leaving home will shelter my mother from any decisions I make about becoming a man. By establishing a time point where I can re-evaluate life, I feel like I'm in control of my destiny. This helps me with the difficult task of refocusing on the big picture.

Not much changes when I return to high school a few weeks later. I'm still taunted for being masculine. Jocks continue to steal my backpack regularly, gloating and tossing it between them. Stares in the girls' locker room remain awkward and I'm constantly objectified by men on the street. But I am at least able to graduate with a profound sense of freedom: an era of torment is over and I can hold on to the hope that I will find others like myself out there waiting.

THE PERFORMANCE

Daniel Vena

"Cellophane / Mister Cellophane / Shoulda been my name / Mister Cellophane / 'Cause you can look right through me / Walk right by me / And never know I'm there . . ."

— "Mr. Cellophane," *Chicago*

I walk out to the center of a darkened stage carrying a white wooden chair. Finding my mark, I stop, gently set down the prop and carefully lower myself onto it. Raising my head, I look out into the crowd as the intermission murmurs fade to a palpable silence. Right on cue the lights rise, unveiling me for the first time.

I wait patiently for a beat, allowing the student-filled audience a moment to survey their next performer. Dressed in a black suit, white French-cuffed shirt and a pink tie, the man seated before them is likely an unexpected addition to a show originally performed as Eve Ensler's *The Vagina Monologues*. Now entitled *Down There*, the event has evolved into an inclusive community-created project raising awareness for various sex, gender, race, religious, size and sexuality-based issues affecting the university. Despite this, it hasn't lost its consistent association with "women's theater." Taking a deep breath, I can feel the weight of this history resting upon me.

I flash the audience a cocky smile, confident they're unsettled by my presence. And then I begin.

63

"I know what you're thinking: how inconsistent! I've
seen women, I've seen female-identified individuals,
I've seen masculine, female-bodied individuals talking
to me about their pussies, about other pussies, about
menstruation, about masturbation, orgasms, frustration, depression, isolation, victimization, hurt, violence
and humiliation. And now look: a man."

Rising, I throw my arms up emphatically.

"A motherfucking man! No sphere he must leave
untouched, no space can be without him—and here he
comes to parade his white, patriarchal power all over
this goddamn stage. I know that's exactly what you
were thinking."

A chuckle ripples through the auditorium, signaling that I've successfully called them out on the first of many assumptions.

"And if you weren't thinking that, you're definitely
thinking: hold on a second, this isn't going to be the gay
man monologue of the night, is it? It's a toss-up in your
head. Is he? Or isn't he?"

I accentuate the final question with a playfully exaggerated lisp,
much to the audience's amusement.

"Okay, let's play with stereotypes. Let's play a game of
catch the questionable homosexual! First at bat, my
likes: Poetry, musicals, baking—which I'm improving on.
Video games, comic books, baseball...well, only when it's
not competitive."

Pausing, I pump my fists with delight.

"Puppies. Long moonlit walks. And yes, I'll own it: I
have a love affair with 1940s melodramas!"

Privately, I'm hoping the audience detects my genuine
enthusiasm.

"Second, let's tackle the physical appearance. Not
Superman, but not too lanky either. A nice unmuscular
middle ground that we shall call 'nerdy chic.' Which is
very in right now, thank God."

A previously abandoned prop bra flies onto the stage amidst claps and catcalls. In an unexpected moment of rock star glory, I absorb what I can of their unconditional support. I'm struck by the bittersweet nature of such a theatrical give-and-take: the more they like me now, the further my eventual fall from grace. I purposely cut their applause short with a small bow before continuing.

> "Tall, but not too tall. Handsome in a delicate way—just
> let me believe that for a moment."

I pause to accept another few hoots and hollers and walk down-stage to direct my gaze at an unsuspecting woman in the front row. Her face registers a look of surprise before offering me a meager smile.

> "Thirdly, let's call into play my profession. Here's the
> kicker, folks: I'm a student. I'm a gender studies major
> with a theater background. And damn if I don't love
> what I do!"

I purposefully elongate the next word, taking my time to strut back to center stage.

> "So an array of things are probably running through
> your head. If you're a straight-identified woman you're
> thinking: A) 'My God, he's perfect!'"

The responding cheers force me to pause for several seconds before I continue.

> "'I wonder if he's single. No, wait! I wonder if he's
> straight and single . . . or if not, I wonder if he has loose
> morals and a free night.'"

A catcaller from the back assures me that this is, indeed, the case.

> "Option B) for all the straight chicks: 'My God, he's
> perfect. Fuck, he's gay!' Which would mean all the gay-
> identified men or wavering bisexuals and pansexuals of
> any gender are probably thinking, 'My God he's perfect...
> hmm, top or bottom?'"

Their laughter swells.

> "Unfortunately, for all the lesbians in the audience, I'm
> probably not your type. However, I do think I am tempt-
> ing one or two of you."

Returning to my chair, I turn it around and straddle the seat, legs opened wide.

> "The overall consensus in the room—at least I would like to believe—is that I, in fact, am the most datable person because I am—yes!—perfect!"

Leaning back, heels kicked up, I cup my hand to my ear.

> "Oh, what was that? Another white man thinking he's perfect? I know, please tell us something we haven't heard before! So now you're thinking, 'Wow, this perfect man seems to be going on a tangent. He's clearly avoiding the question! Is he or isn't he?'"

I take a measured breath and repeat each syllable precisely.

> *"Is he or isn't he? Well,"*

I continue, stepping towards the front row,

> "Let's take a little survey."

With one hand pressed against the floor for balance, I leap off the stage and into the audience.

> "Show of hands: who thinks I am gay?"

No one participates. For the first time, I see all their faces clearly. Many share an expression of overwhelming confusion. I've disrupted the pattern. I'm not supposed to stand down here and demand an answer to my question. So I try again with a more playful tone.

> "Who thinks I'm a flaming homosexual?"

A young male audience member shyly puts his hand up. Flirtatiously I reply,

> "You hoping so, honey?"

He blushes.

> "And show of hands: who thinks I'm not?"

More hands shoot up. I wonder momentarily if they think this answer is less offensive to me. Perhaps they imagine my ego or, more importantly, my masculinity won't be sorely affected by this conclusion. I move on.

> "Excellent. Now who's still bloody confused about the point of all this?"

A middle-aged man throws up his hand. I immediately turn to meet his gaze and deliver my next scripted line.

> "Yes, there's always the slow audience members, aren't there?"

The woman beside him lets out a snort and he slowly lowers his hand, twisting his face into a self-mocking pout.

> "But to be fair, I'm purposefully being snarky. I'm strategically leaving the goal of this whole line of questioning a little bit ambiguous."

I turn to ascend the stage stairs and resume sitting.

> "For the most part I'm just curious as to how you perceive my sexuality—which is deliciously flamboyant, isn't it? Except, of course, for the fact that I exclusively sleep with women."

Leaning forward, I mouth the next word.

> "Shocking. But the question 'Is he or isn't he,' which everyone seems to ask, now erases another bigger question that *no one* even thinks to ask."

Standing tall, feet firmly planted, I take a deep breath.

> "Is he a *he* or isn't he?"

If it's possible, the room falls even more silent than the moment before. I notice one woman clasp her hand to her mouth; another leans forward in her chair, waiting anxiously for my next line.

> "You see, the point of this Shakespeare-inspired, egotistical, narcissistic rampage is not to prove how self-centered men are, but to create one giant red herring. My life—or at least my gender—has become one giant red herring because everyone assumes I'm a 'biological' man."

I hear a murmur or two, but the rapid beating of my heart muffles the words.

> "And by saying this I've now somehow invited you to look more closely at me. You may notice I don't have an Adam's apple and that there's just the slightest curve to my hips."

I trace my hand down my waist.

"Well, I'll bite. I'll be the monkey in the cage for a moment. Go on, give me a good once over. See anything you like?"

Someone—I can't tell who—begins to snicker but is immediately shushed by another audience member sitting close by.

"Think you have me all figured out now? No. No, you're probably more confused than ever. And to be honest... so am I."

I hang my head and compose myself. Picking it back up I say,

"Look, I'll be frank with you. I'm not a tough or sexy guy. I don't curse. I typically don't say 'pussy' even inside the bedroom. And it's taking all the effort I can muster not to pass out from being the center of attention, which I actually hate. But we all have to tough it out sometimes. We all tough it out because we all want to be noticed. Whether we want to be recognized by the world or one special person—or two or three, depending on how kinky you are—we just want somebody, anybody, to see us for all that we are."

I walk forward to the stage's edge.

"If you're a musical fan you'll know *Chicago* and you'll definitely know the character Amos. Amos sings the classic song, 'Mr. Cellophane'—which I will not sing because I don't want your ears to bleed."

I get a few indulgent giggles.

"The song is about being invisible. And I'll admit, sometimes I feel completely cellophane: that my past life never happened; that no one actually sees me for who I am."

With each passing moment I lose confidence in my ability to withstand the audience's penetrating gaze. Their once adoring faces now carry looks of judgment or maybe it's just my imagination. To deal with the uncertainty and settle my shaking body, I rationalize my vulnerability as a necessary acting exercise. All good performers lay their heart bare on the stage. *How ironic*, I think. Perhaps biography and fiction are never quite separate.

> "Of course, you could say I did it to myself. I take the hormones; I had the surgery. I pass. I get it. And I know I've been really fortunate when it comes to passing and having white privilege, that I haven't experienced violence, that no one bats an eye at me. I know."

I inhale sharply, readying my most commanding voice.

> "And let me add that passing is not the 'be-all-end-all' of transitioning. The very term screams *problematic*. It is not our problem to resemble 'legible' men and women. It's society's problem to redefine its infuriatingly tiny boxes of what is and isn't acceptable!"

Low but audible, I hear several affirmative hollers echo throughout the theater.

> "I get how people read me. They see man. Just man. But sometimes...sometimes I wish they could just know."

I drop my voice, tugging at my jacket.

> "Know how complex I am, know how complex my body is. For fuck's sake, I'm apparently a walking Frankenstein and I want some goddamn recognition for the journey I've made every once and awhile without having to constantly think of polite and charming ways to out myself!"

I recall the numerous clever one-liners I've perfected to explain my "difference" to dates, employers or friends. It must be so much lighter to walk around without these catch-all phrases in your back pocket.

> "Listen, this isn't some sob story about a poor little white trans guy who can't cope with his life of privilege. This is about not being able to be recognized as I am, in my entirety. This is about transitioning only to find I still don't 'fit' anywhere."

I watch the spit fly from my mouth. I want my diction to be as precise as possible as I let the next words land.

"This is about the looks of disgust I get at lesbian bars when all I want to do is scream out 'I was one of you!' This is about losing access to the women's washroom and the fact that no guy wants to talk while peeing."

Some chuckle uncomfortably; others shift their legs awkwardly in their seats.

"This is about the mother who looks at me sideways while walking with her daughter, thinking I'm a threat to both of them. Or about the guy at the video store who calls me 'boss' or 'bro' as if I am his confidant in masculinity. This is about losing a sense of home and feeling like a transient outsider everywhere I go. This is about the perpetual search to find a safe space for myself. But you know what?"

I calm myself, holding up an index finger.

"Being here, ranting and raving—this feels good. This feels safe. So thank you. Thank you each and every one of you. Thank you for giving me a ten-minute home. And most of all, thank you for helping peel away my cellophane wrapping."

I give a gracious, subtle bow. As I come up, the audience breaks into applause, continuing even after I walk off the stage. I take a breath filled with relief and wonder if I've been *heard*, or merely listened to.

—•—

After several more monologues, the actors pour out of the green room to meet their loved ones. Immediately, I'm approached by a group of students, all sporting the university's athletics jacket. One by one they offer me their hands and congratulate me on the show.

After an exchange of pleasantries, one of the women nonchalantly asks, "So, how much research did you do for your role?" A man who had moments earlier been eyeing me up-and-down, adds, "Yeah, because seriously you were born a dude. Right?"

I sink down as I realize the irony: in their eyes, I'm still not trans. Even after baring my soul, my life story, I'm nothing but an actor—and a cissexual one at that—playing a part.

In my distress I evade the question, stutter out an awkward good-bye and return defeated to the green room to pack my belongings. My mind swirls as I count the number of performances I've completed tonight. I am the self-as-performer and the actor-as-self; I am a trans-sexual masquerading as a cissexual and a cissexual playing a transsex-ual. I am a fabrication of research and I am a body of experience. The lines become so blurred that the once seemingly interesting decision to not—unlike others in the show—announce my piece as autobio-graphical is now a lost opportunity for clarification. I remain without definition.

Looking into the dressing room mirror, I watch as I unfasten my own cufflinks. As I do, my mind's eye returns to the theater. It's empty now. A single light illuminates center stage. I step forward, finding my mark. I deliver lines I have never said aloud but, perhaps somewhere inside, have always rehearsed.

> "To the individuals who approached me after the show, you will never know what you stole from me tonight. In this society, trans individuals are rarely allowed to be authentic. We are always 'fakes' or 'copies' of 'real' men and women. But atop this stage, I had become real. And your words erased that. You stripped me of meaning so that I may exist in a way more understandable to you."

I begin to undo my shirt buttons, stripping away layer after layer until I lay myself bare.

> "I was seen not for who I am, but for who you wanted me to be. I became a simple actor conditioned to rehearse lines given to me, not by my own lived experi-ence, but by a piece of paper someone else had writ-ten on. You judged me solely on the 'authenticity' of

my 'act.' And here, just like in life, I passed. I passed so extraordinarily well that you were willing to dismiss the truth I was revealing. Instead, you chose to fabricate a story and shove me into it. I will say this only once: I am not a part of your lie."

The lights fade.

PART II
FAMILY MAN

FAMILY MAN

Aaron H. Devor

I can still remember standing in the corner of the kitchen, looking out the window onto the backyard and driveway where I shot hoops with the local boys. I was talking on the phone with one of my best girlfriends—one of those old wall phones with an actual dial and separate handset attached by a curly cord. I think it was yellow.

I was talking in hushed tones in case my mother came into the room. What I was saying was scary and dangerous: I was telling her I was a lesbian in a time when no one knew anyone who was a lesbian. This was before Stonewall, in a time when kids like me got sent to mental hospitals for being gay. Kids were given shock treatments to straighten them out.

My friend took it okay: we could still be friends. In fact, we still are friends. One of the first things that we talked about was how it meant that I wouldn't ever have kids, that I'd never have a family of my own.

Even then it brought tears to my eyes. It seemed like a big price to pay, but that's the way it was back then. You were lucky to grow up at all if you were gay. You were doing well if you had any kind of decent life where at least a few people *knew*, and were okay with it. I just resigned myself to the idea that I'd never have kids or a family.

As the years went by, lots of things changed. Lesbians and gays didn't have to hide so much anymore. People like me—and eventually me—built successful and out, even mainstream, lives. Lesbians and gays had babies and built their own families.

I could see this all happening around me, but I wasn't *that* kind of lesbian. I was far too butch, far too manly, to ever consider having a baby. And neither I, nor the women in my life, were ready to start a family while we were still young enough to do so.

So I grew up and into maturity getting attached to other people's kids, never having a primary relationship with any of them. When people asked, as they will do from time to time, whether I had any regrets in life, I replied that I only had one: I'd never had my own kids. I'd quickly explain that it wasn't that I felt I had made any wrong choices, it was just that I couldn't bear to be a mother and regretted that I'd never had the chance to be a father.

Now, everything has changed.

———

Today, I am a husband, a son-in-law, a brother, an uncle and great uncle, a (step)father and a grandfather. (But not a son or grandson. My parents and grandparents are already gone.) Of course, my transition was pivotal, but it was a very slow pivot. All of us grew into these new roles together. We knew that the words for our relationships officially changed with my gender documentation, but the actual relationships each moved at their own pace.

My father-in-law was probably the fastest—pretty much instantaneous. My wife, Lynn, and I had been married by our rabbi in a same-sex wedding at our home several years before, and we'd already been together for more than a decade at that point. Lynn's parents had been accepting, but never entirely comfortable, with our same-sex relationship. When I sat down with my father-in-law to tell him that I was going to transition, tears came to his eyes—the only time I've ever seen him weep—and he gave me his blessings.

According to Lynn, his behavior around us changed immediately, as soon as we joined her and her mother for dinner in the next room. Before, he had mostly addressed his comments on business, politics, fishing and the environment to his eldest and most intellectual child: my wife, Lynn. As soon as he had another man in the room, Lynn felt that she had been shunted aside. He wanted to talk man-to-man. For a few years the womenfolk were relegated to spectators on most subjects, but now things have evened out more.

Over the years, he and I have gradually grown into that father/son relationship. My own dad had been gone for more than thirty years so I had a gap that wanted filling. My father-in-law has two sons of his own but they live far, and farther, away; Lynn and I live close enough to see her folks often.

In recent years, trips to see Lynn's parents have become almost weekly for me, and almost daily for my wife. My father-in-law has taken me under his wing in a gentle and kindly way, passing on his wisdom and a few of his treasured possessions. He has begun to accept a little help from me as he's started losing some mobility with age.

But I think most importantly for me, as an otherwise fatherless (and motherless) son, is that he has taken fatherly pride in my accomplishments. I've come to feel that I do, again, have a father who cares about me, supports me in my dreams, cheers me in my successes, and trusts me with his first-born child, on whom he now depends for so much.

It means a lot to me to feel that I have his respect and caring. I feel that I am a son for the first time in my life, and that feels right and good. So I try to do my part without usurping those born to the role.

My only and older brother lives quite far away and we see each other about once a year. He has probably been the slowest to come to a new relationship with me. After all, he grew up and had many decades with me as his little sister. I doubt he sees it from my perspective: that a lot about our relationship had been brother-like all along.

He was supportive of my transition from the start. When I told him I was changing, the first thing he said was "Well, just make sure that you do it safe." He learned pretty quickly to use my correct name. Pronouns took a lot longer, and he still slips sometimes.

It was over a decade before I heard him comfortably introduce me to someone as his brother. I never pushed him on it. I just waited for him to change his way of talking about me. After all, he had a lifetime of habits to unlearn. Language, while important, is only a small part of our relationship. What is far more important is that we have become closer with the passing of the years. We're comfortable with each other. We want to spend time together, and it is easy and warm when we do.

Would that have happened simply with the passage of time? Who knows? Certainly we did a lot of relationship healing after our mother (and last parent) died and we realized that, if we didn't care for each other, we'd have no reason to ever see each other again. I feel like we've both come to better understand what is important in life; family is very high on both of our lists.

However, I also know that "when you conclude the war in your own head, you are free to make peace with the rest of the world."[1] Having found peace in my head and heart, I think that I have become easier to be around. I think that he, too, has mellowed with age. We both feel the need for each other much more these days. I feel blessed to have his love.

He has two sons who were both pretty much grown by the time I transitioned. As far as I could tell, we all just moved into our new relationships seamlessly. I suspect that I never made much sense to them as a female anyway and it was just easier when I finally got it right.

One of my nephews has married and they have a brand new daughter. To her, I will always have been Great Uncle Aaron. I suppose that one day she'll want to ask some questions. I imagine that by the time that happens, the fact that I am trans will just be a mundane detail of an old man's biography, and of pretty minimal interest to a young girl.

———

Being a father is something that I thought that I had missed out on for sure. By the time Lynn and I got together, her son was already grown and her tubes were tied. She'd had him early in life and he'd been raised by his father and stepmom.

When I came into Lynn's life, her son had recently graduated high school and had come to live with his mom in the big city. Sadly, he also came with a serious drinking problem, which persisted and progressed over the next decade.

When Lynn moved in with me, her son stayed in the same city as us and moved on with the kind of chaotic and self-destructive life that alcoholism brings with it. We worried about him and rescued him from self-inflicted danger or injury far too many times.

We tried everything we could to convince him that he was on a suicidal course. Finally we refused him access to us when he was drunk—which was most of the time—and anxiously awaited the next late-night call from the hospital or police. I was there, sharing the crisis and drama, but still as his mother's partner, not any kind of father.

I think that started to change when he phoned one day, drunk and sick again, asking to come over. We relented and let him sleep it off on the couch. He was unconscious for days.

I'll never forget the afternoon that he finally got off the couch and was trying to drink some juice at the kitchen counter. His hands shook so hard that he could barely take a sip. That was when he asked us what day it was. When we told him, he realized that he'd been out for three days.

"If I don't stop drinking, it's going to kill me," he finally said. Of course, we'd been telling him that for years and he'd been denying that he had a problem.

He stayed with us for the next year. We made a room for him and fed him and I paid many of his living expenses while he got clean. In the fifteen years since that day, he's never taken another drink.

———

My (step)son and I didn't talk deeply during the year he stayed in our house, mostly just day-to-day things. Still, we lived together as a family. We came to know each other, starting a relationship that was not father/son, but began to have a familial feel to it. Then things moved to a new level: his partner got pregnant and he needed to prepare himself to be a father.

He had a lot of unresolved anger about his mother not raising him and he decided to deal with it then. He didn't want to bring that into his relationship with his own kid. In retrospect, I think that before he could start to accept me as a fatherly-type person in his life—especially since he has his own birth father, who raised him and whom he sees from time-to-time—he needed to make peace with his feelings about his mother. As it is for most of us, that's an ongoing process.

Over the years, he's needed me to talk both with him and with his mom as a mediator and interpreter when things have gotten hot between them. As he's come to see that I care about him and about their relationship, that I don't always take Lynn's side and that I see him pretty clearly too, we've grown closer. The trust has grown.

Now, we talk. We have our own visits. We have our own relationship. He turns to me sometimes when he's sorting things out with his mom, with his ex-wife, about his ex-wife's daughter, about his son. I hope that he feels about me somewhat how I feel about my father-in-law.

I care from the heart about him. I celebrate his successes and feel for him when he hurts. I'm honored that he sometimes comes to me for advice, and I try to give him my best. Maybe all of that would have happened anyway. However, I think that I can understand his challenges and dilemmas better from my perspective as a man. And I think that he can trust that I understand and empathize with him better now that I am a man.

———

Never having expected to be a father, being a grandfather is its own little miracle. In my case it takes two forms: one simple and sweet, the other complex and somewhat tortured. I'll start with the hard part. When our son got together with his now ex-wife, she already had a daughter from a previous relationship. The girl was a sweet little five-year-old when she came into our lives.

Back then, they lived a short walk away from us and we saw a lot of the girl. She'd stay overnight with us at least once a week and there was a lot of back-and-forthing between scheduled visits. She never called us her grandparents then; she had two sets already.

During those years I transitioned, but we never had a conversation with her about it. We simply carried on. My body changed as she watched. One day everyone started calling me Aaron. A few months later, she did too—and that was that. We were just there in her life as we grew to be her family too.

When she became a preteen, and a year-and-a-half after her brother was born, her family moved seven hundred and fifty miles away from us. Visits dwindled to a week or so a few times a year and we kept in touch on the phone as best we could.

Simultaneously, things became very sore between our son and her mom as they ended their relationship. It was a rough time for everyone: things were said, things were done, and everyone got hurt.

Knowing what we did about the mom, we foresaw that her daughter would end up on our doorstep one day asking for refuge. We figured she would run away, but that's not how it actually happened. It was her mother who asked her to not return home when she was fourteen-and-a-half and out of the house visiting her biological dad. That was when our (ex-step)granddaughter called and asked to come live with us.

We took her in, neither of us ever having raised a child before—let alone a troubled teenaged girl. As we tried to raise that very hurting teenager, I became a grandfather.

I'm not convinced that she thought of me as her grandfather before that, but she had to tell her friends at school *something*. "Grandparents" was the closest she could come to a sensible description of who we were to her. It was an odd *in loco parentis* dance we did for the year-and-a-half that she lived with us.

She was angry from having grown up in survival mode in a chaotic environment ever since she was tiny. Her values and way of relating to other people were about managing to get by in an unpredictable, unfair, and dangerous world.

As the man of the house, my job kicked in when I was home after work and on the weekends. Mostly I served as ballast for the emotional whirlwind that developed when Lynn, her day-to-day caregiver, tried to provide a troubled, high-drama, hormone-fueled, teenage girl the first structure, stability, and consistency she had ever known.

I was largely excluded from all of the quiet and warm intimate girl talk about bodies and boys. I was spared some of the tear-filled hysterics, but just as often I was called upon to mediate, moderate, and sometimes to adjudicate.

Together, Lynn and I learned a lot about parenting, and our girl started to learn that there are some people in the world who say what they mean and mean what they say—that some people can be counted upon to be consistent, fair, kind, and even generous at times. In the process, we all stretched and grew immensely.

After a year-and-a-half with us, her mother wanted her back and she went, hoping that things would be different. It wasn't, but *she* was, and we were as well. We were her family now too. Within months, things went badly again, but this time our girl pushed back, and so did we. The ensuing truce only lasted a few months.

Now she's gone to live with her biological dad, with whom she had never lived before, and who has also never raised any kids before. Things have been rough there too. I've reached out to her dad with fatherly support when his own dad was not able to do so. We've built a bond.

It has been hard to see this girl suffer and act out so much. She's tried to do well in school, and to get along with people, but she's not been taught all the skills that she needs. While I made some pretty major sacrifices in my career to be able to take her in when we did, it was worth it. I am grateful to have her in my life, grateful to have been able to build that relationship and to give her a glimpse that life can be better than the chaos in which she routinely wraps herself.

Now our girl is just about to launch into her own adult life. None of us adults think that she is ready, so I expect that there will be lots more parenting/grandparenting to do for many years to come. We have built a bond that will last our lives and I cherish that I—who never thought that I would have kids—now have a granddaughter.

———

Our grandson is still young enough that he has always been a simple joy to me. For reasons that still elude and amaze me, we have a very special bond. When he was too little to know better, he'd even say embarrassing things about wanting to live with us forever.

When he stays with us now, he's so overwhelmingly focused on following me around and doing everything that I do that Lynn has to struggle with feelings of jealousy. When I'm at work he asks all day long, "When is Zeyda coming home?"[2]

We roughhouse, we play outdoors, and I read him to sleep every night. In the mornings, we have cuddles in bed and intimate talks until he explodes into raucous boy-child energy. He eats breakfast out of my bowl and has learned to use kid-sized chopsticks that I brought back for him from China, just so he can be like me. He sits next to me at every meal. I play superheroes with him during bath time. He's still young enough that he trusts me in every way. He still wants to cuddle and sit on my lap and hold my hand, and it melts my heart to goo. He is this unequivocally shining light in my life.

I lock away a small niggling fear that one day he will be disappointed to find out that I am trans, and that he will turn away from me because of it. By the time that happens—which could be today—I'm hoping that the reality of our relationship will be enough to carry us through. Meanwhile, I continue to love him and bask in his simple childish devotion. Now I am a grandfather and some kind of role model for a sweet little boy. My heart sings.

Having Lynn love me through so many years, and so many changes, has given me much more than I can begin to describe in this short essay. What I can say is that she has brought with her a spectrum of family that has enriched my life in ways that go beyond the words that I have. For that, I am profoundly grateful.

Being trans has allowed me to mostly heal that one place in my life where I ever really felt regret. While it is still true that I will never have or raise "kids of my own," I am now intensely enmeshed in an extended family, in profoundly meaningful relationships where I am the right version of me: husband, brother, son-in-law, stepfather, grandfather. Now, it is up to me to perform those roles with all the honor, respect, kindness, and dignity that they deserve and that this man can muster.

SCULPTOR

Willy Wilkinson

When I was in middle school, my father endeavored to whittle away the stressful demands of the workplace, so he enrolled in a night class on woodcarving. It began with a challenging task: to take a small rectangular piece of soft plywood and carve a ball, round as possible, within a frame. A ball in cage, if you will.

The ball had to be able to roll within the four corners of the frame, yet it could not get too small or it would fall out. The trick was in taking away just enough to create the round shape, yet leaving the material necessary for its containment. I watched his quiet demeanor and focus slowly reveal the spherical form, and the thrill and pride as his thumb pushed the ball in motion without escape. I was impressed at the transformation of this nondescript piece of wood into a dynamic and seemingly impossible creation.

His next task was to whittle a wooden chain from a cylindrical stick of plywood, again shedding what was unnecessary but leaving enough to keep the chain intact. Crudely executed yet smooth to the touch, the oval links inextricably interconnected themselves like a strand of DNA or the linkages of life, solidifying my father's destiny as a fine wood sculptor.

At this time, I often tossed a football with my Dad, refining my spiral and even winning a physical education award in seventh grade for my skill. My best buddy was Susan, a female-bodied person who, in retrospect, seemed trans masculine, though she may not identify that way even today. She embodied a strong male energy and was confident, smart and sometimes overbearing. Caucasian and stocky with short brown hair, she stretched a boy's white T-shirt and blue plaid button-down shirt over her large, early developing breasts.

Susan was my pal who understood my gender without explanation, like the girls we chased and goofed with. We did well in school, wore our boy's shirts and watched football on her big color TV in her mansion of a house. Her mom, raised rich from Texas oil money, transported me home daily from school, along with her two kids, in a large wood-paneled station wagon, the 70s mini-van of choice.

But Wednesdays were different. That was the day our seventh grade social studies teacher had a standing substitute, Mrs. Winkleberg's, who dodged many a spitball in our gifted-class chaos. On Mrs. Winkelberg's first day, Susan became Steve, and I, already Willy, enjoyed trying to fool her into thinking that we were guys as we put our arms around our stand-in girlfriends, who seemed to enjoy the fun.

Wednesdays were also the day my Mom picked me up in our tried-and-true Dodge Dart and bribed me with the rare treat of McDonald's cheeseburgers and chocolate milkshakes before Chinese School. Though I have always loved learning languages and have a knack for it, I continually struggled with being in the milieu of Chinese people honoring our linguistic and cultural traditions.

"Eyes on the board and repeat after me," the teacher ordered sternly. Along with the hands-folded obedience she demanded and a disciplinary approach that was heavy with shame and scorn, there were clear gender expectations, which meant that I was supposed to be a good Chinese girl—quiet, respectful and eager to obey.

I imagined the arcs of spitballs headed in the teacher's direction, but instead did what I and all the other students were raised to do: follow directions, do the homework and have the right answers. Though I felt a certain kinship with the few kids in my age range, I also felt ruffled by them. They were the people I was trying so hard not to be—awkward nerds ridiculed for their fashion expressions, lunch food, intelligence and introversion. Their proximity pushed my internalized racism buttons, and made Chinese School emotionally wrenching for me. Though I actually enjoyed mastering such written and spoken gems as, "The cow went up the mountain. The sheep went down the mountain," I felt caught between my Mom's insistence that I attend and my own inner conflict of owning my heritage.

"It's Winky Dink and Chinky Dink Day, Wilkinson," Susan informed me every Wednesday in her caustic, amused tone. That meant that I wouldn't be carpooling with her that day, of course. It was also a reminder that that's who I was, a Chink headed to Chinky Dink School. I wanted to whittle away the part of me that got called "Chink" but keep the container, the part that was a boy.

———

On one weekend, out with my parents, we ran into a pleasant co-worker of my father's.

"Oh, this must be one of your sons," she acknowledged warmly.

"Uhh...yes," stammered my father, "this is my son," and then inserted my girl name for comic effect.

As soon as the co-worker was out of earshot, my exasperated mother angrily announced, "I thought we had three daughters!" I wanted to sculpt myself into the boy I always knew I was meant to be.

My father knows wood like an extension of his hands, rough logs transformed into the gentle graces of a woman's curves or the fearless leap of a dancer. He begins by turning the wood in his palms, examining its every twist and blemish, then shaves away and refines its natural beauty into a new form that was already there, intrinsic. While some work originates from fallen tree branches, other pieces are carefully selected for the wood's properties. But no matter the source, they all get sculpted into fine art, diligently sanded to a smooth caress and stained to deep, rich tones.

As a young adult I began to sculpt, first focusing my efforts on the internal framework before venturing to carve and sand the rough exterior terrain. My psyche grew like a gnarled tree on the Pacific Coast, the stiff ocean winds pushing, pulling, wrenching, twisting it into its unique form, outstretched arms, jagged and vibrant.

Decades later, in puberty for the second time and still sculpting, I jump into a massive outdoor pool and slice the water until I push back the shame, the violent gaze, the racism and all the insidious barriers to my being. I build my pecs and I am stronger in my ability to stand tall with my chest out. The girth of my neck expands to hold the weight of all the noise in my head. My legs thicken so I can walk the extra mile. I shed the subjugation of being an Asian female in this society so I can present myself as the proud Asian man that I am: a husband, brother, father.

But somehow I am not the only one at the chisel. I feel the expert hands of others sculpting me into being, the wooden chain of interconnectedness. I sense the rough, crooked hands of my *haole* father in his shop and the brown, smooth hands of my uncles mixing *mah jongg* tiles. I sense my father's father in dark blue overalls tinkering in his woodshed and my mother's father sitting on the ground weaving baskets from coconut palm fronds. And I feel how my three children, ages seven, four and one, shape me into the Dad that I am, as I divide my time between working long hours as a public health consultant and caring for them in a daily way.

At a party with my family, my four-year-old daughter runs to me, smiling broadly, giggling, arms outstretched, and jumps into mid-air as I bend to catch her, lifting her high into the sky, spinning her around and around, legs horizontal, like a helicopter in flight. We are one, twirling in joy, smiling to our ears and laughing as we dance to the music. I am there to catch them, comfort and teach them, walk hand-in-hand with them, protect them. They sculpt me with their certainty that I will catch them and hold them as the father I am today.

Engrossed on my computer in my home office, from time to time I drop to do fifty push-ups, to sculpt the arms that carry my sleeping children into our home and the shoulders that bear the financial burden of supporting a family of five. I tone and hone my torso into the male physique I was meant to have, releasing the past and reveling in the present.

My father's rugged hands caress the finely sanded, beautifully stained figure of a person in flight, arms outstretched, jumping into the unknown, the ball in a cage and the wooden chain long lost in time but not forgotten.

BECOMING ABA

Nathan Ezekiel

When my daughter Leigh was a baby, I loved "New Moms" groups. I knew the entire local circuit: which store, church or synagogue to hit on which day to find a friendly gathering of exhausted parents and infants. I knew which groups had snacks and which had an occasional dad in attendance. Back then I was "Mama."

I had spent much of my wife Gail's pregnancy fearing I wouldn't find a solid place in our family. Who would I be to a child I hadn't carried, birthed or nursed and with whom I shared no genetic link? What would she gain by having me in her family? Even the materials directed specifically to lesbian non-bio-moms sent a clear message that, at best, I was a kind of bonus parent—nice to have around, but by no means essential. I didn't need to be the primary parent to the exclusion of Gail, but I needed to *matter*.

Once Leigh was in my arms, she and I started to build our relationship and my fears began to subside. When I bundled her up to head out to the "New Moms" groups, the easy acceptance I found there, recognized unquestioningly as my daughter's parent, was a welcome balm for any last worries about whether I had a meaningful part to play in her life.

Once there, I also felt a surprising alignment with womanhood. In the past, I had primarily joined social groups of women that served as refuges within male-dominated subcultures. As a scientist and mathematician, I sought connections with women who understood what it was like to face sexism every day, both subtle and overt—women who understood the fatigue that comes from so often being "the only one." I fit into these groups in part because we were all working somewhat counter to what was expected based on gender.

In contrast, I fit into moms' groups because I was doing exactly what was expected of me as a woman: caring for my baby. Though initially a bit mystified, I learned to fit in, dialing back the direct, occasionally brash communication style I'd cultivated as a scientist working primarily among men. As I adjusted, I experienced a strange lightness; it was easy, almost intoxicating, to slip into a culturally sanctioned space, to do these tasks for which I had blanket societal permission.

The friendships I made in these groups were mostly with moms, both straight and queer, who were doing the lion's share of direct parenting work in their families. But as Leigh grew, Gail and I developed our strongest friendships with mom-dad families in which parents intentionally shared in the daily care of their children. Through these dads, who I saw building central and positive roles in the lives of their kids, I began to understand that motherhood was not a prerequisite for the kind of parenthood I sought.

———

When our daughter is about a year old, I begin to pursue my own pregnancy with focus and raw determination. Though we'd always planned on two children, I'm also driven by a desire to somehow "fix" my body.

It's difficult to place what *exactly* I'm seeking to remedy. I reason that after sixteen years of long, painful and irregular periods, I just want my body to work like it's supposed to. I'd previously spent years on multiple risky and unnecessary medications, then additional years of weaning off them. Pregnancy can be a benchmark: proof that my body made it through that gauntlet intact.

But it's more than that. I'd always carried a deep sense that my body was fundamentally flawed in some crucial, undefined way. Like many of the feelings before I consciously understood my maleness, this becomes most clear when examined in relief, as a reverse image of the comfort I embody now.

As we had prepared for Leigh's arrival, I had become immersed in the culture and mythology surrounding childbirth, intrigued by what I learned from our close friend and midwife. Approaching my own pregnancy, I hold tight to the idea that carrying and birthing a child are amazing spiritual and physical experiences. I believe I'll feel like the most powerful person in the world, connected to every woman for all time, tapped into the deepest soul of the universe. I want that. I *need* that. Surely if I can do something so powerful, this one thing my body is meant to do, my unrest—this feeling of being physically misplaced and fundamentally broken—will disappear.

As it turns out, my pregnancy and labor are physically grueling: I'm constantly nauseated and suffering from pain that makes walking and toddler-handling nearly impossible. Even so, I experience a moment in the second trimester, after I've finally stopped vomiting and the aches have faded, when I think, "This is it. I'm finally a healthy pregnant lady! Now must be when it gets really good."

But almost as soon as I can rest, my skin begins to itch incessantly, especially on my hands, legs and feet, soon escalating to a point where sleep and coherent thought are impossible. My homebirth midwife quickly realizes this is a sign of a rare and risky liver complication called *intrahepatic cholestasis of pregnancy* and transfers me to my back-up obstetrician. In order to avoid the substantial risk of stillbirth, my labor needs to be induced in the hospital several weeks early.

After an arduous three-day labor with no pain medication, I give birth to Ira, a healthy baby boy. While I emerge from this challenge with a profound understanding of my own strength and another great kid, it's not the transformation I had been hoping for. The sense that something still isn't right persists and gradually deepens.

About a year after Ira's birth, layered within our ongoing conversations about queerness, I say to Gail, "If I were younger, I think things might have been different. I think I might have been trans." She listens, but we both brush it off, agreeing the world is different now than when we came out in the '90s.

In some ways, I have always known I am male. The insight, however, has taken many forms and conscious awareness has been fleeting. As a child, there were times I understood and thought perhaps the adults around me had made a mistake. There were moments in my late teens, especially when I first understood myself as queer, when I *knew* consciously, but couldn't see a possible path forward. I chose to forget and make do.

Now in my mid-thirties, my reawakening starts with shopping—or, rather, with Gail's shopping. Frustrated with a frumpy wardrobe unchanged throughout five years of parenting, she vows to spend $50 on clothes every month. Bit-by-bit she comes home with stylish new outfits. She cuts her hair and begins putting more effort into her look each morning. I'm surprised to find that something about this unsettles me: she's choosing items I would never wear.

I had thought we had the same taste in clothing. But when she comes home with her latest flowing scarf, flowered jacket or brightly colored shirt, I can't imagine myself wearing any of them. I stick to my usual mundane, worn-out attire for six months, until my competitive spirit kicks in and I decide I can meet her challenge: $50 a month, come hell or high water.

My early shopping trips share a defining feature: blinding rage. Angrily flipping through racks in the women's section, all I can think is, "These are so hideous. I can't believe anyone buys this crap." Every now and then I find something just dull enough to be tolerable and reach my $50 minimum. Growing curious about whether I might fare better in the men's department, I hatch a plan to shop with one of my closest friends, Jesse, a trans man who's almost my size.

It works like a charm. I come home from our weekend shopping trip with men's clothing I look forward to wearing. When I peer into the mirror that evening, I experience a jolt of recognition. I start ironing my clothes, eagerly laying out my slacks and button-downs every night, planning for the next day.

After that first taste, I gradually feel my way towards manhood, as if grasping in the dark for something I desperately need but am also scared to find. How can I explain the unfolding understanding? It feels like a dawning realization that my life until this point has been lived in black-and-white, but that there's a whole other life available that I can live in color. That who I am in my body, and in relation to my wife's body, does not have to be what I had always thought.

I experience those first steps—my shifting wardrobe, binding, tentative changes in my sexual relationship with Gail, the moment I know my name, the first time I hear "he"—as brief, brilliant flashes of recognition. They are moments of sudden, exhilarating respite from a longstanding dull and deep ache, like having a headache for so long you've almost forgotten you have it until suddenly, one day, it's just gone.

At first, Gail and I live our new life—the one in which I might be a man—only after the kids go to bed and on the occasional night out. I talk to her as my understanding shifts, almost as soon as the thoughts and feelings occur. Even though we are both confused and overwhelmed, we establish a stronger connection with each step I make towards inhabiting my maleness. After more than ten years together, we're falling in love all over again.

It's exhilarating to take up residence in my body after decades of absence, but also terrifying to feel the discomfort and pain I've pushed away for so long. After taking off my binder at night I toss and turn, struggling to find enough peace in my body to fall asleep.

I look back over my life and feel anew anguish I had thought was long past. I mentally revisit my childhood hope that I would never grow up, my fear and desperation during puberty. I see with new eyes the former confusion about my sexual identity—my clear attraction to women but difficulty enjoying sex in a body I understood as female, my longstanding fantasies centered on straight sex. I feel as if I'm coming apart at the seams, even as I tap into a powerful core self.

—•—

Part of me still hopes this is all limited in scope: that maybe it's only about sex or something private about my body. Maybe if I just change a couple of things, I can still be "Mama." By now our kids are ages five and two and I tell myself I need to know my path for certain before I reveal anything to them. I'm still searching for a way to avoid turning their world upside down. Then they start an argument.

Around the dinner table one night, our son begins confidently reviewing who is who, addressing Gail first. "Ima is a woman. Leigh is a girl. I am a boy. Mama is a man."

"No, she is not! Mama is a woman! Ima, tell him! Tell him he's wrong!" Leigh exclaims.

"No! Mama is a *man!*" Ira shouts and back and forth it goes. Gail and I lock eyes like deer caught in headlights. I'm not ready to claim my male identity or to acknowledge the reality that I will medically transition.

"I'm kind of some of each," I manage to choke out. My daughter's jaw drops, but the conversation moves on. Later, I ask her if she knew what I'd meant.

"Yes, Mama, I understand," she replies. "You like to wear man clothes, but you are a woman and *you want to stay a woman.*" Her last phrase comes accompanied by a stony glare.

She's already learned from Jesse that some people are assigned female at birth but know that they are male and sometimes change their bodies. When she declares that I will *stay a woman*, she confirms what I had merely suspected after the dinnertime debate: she's considered that I might transition.

The next night, Leigh comes home still chewing on this news. She's vibrating with questions, some she can form and others she cannot.

"Are you going to change your name?" she starts.

"Some people who feel like I do change their name, but I don't know yet," I answer.

"But what will our friends think?" she persists.

"Our friends love us very much and they'll still love us just as much." I feel grateful to know that this is absolutely true.

She continues to slip in and out of the conversation; she flails her arms and cackles with laughter; she desperately makes up silly jokes. I hold her. I manage not to cry.

"But can I still call you Mama?" she wonders.

"I don't know," I respond. "You can right now." Then I remind her how much I love her and that she will always be my kid no matter what.

After I put her to bed I sob, broken that I might ask this of my children. At the time, I can only see that I must be hurting them.

———

A month later we tell Leigh that Gail will be calling me by a new name and saying "he." Although our daughter is vocally opposed, she also clamors for my attention. She toys with what to call me, pointedly juxtaposing my previous and current names then laughing awkwardly. She suggests lists of gender-neutral alternatives and recites names she wants to have instead of her own.

"I don't want to talk about it with anyone, ever," she declares. But by the end of the day she runs inside excitedly, leaving her neighborhood friend standing on the sidewalk.

"Mama, can I tell Rose all about it? Can I tell her your new name and about how you're changing?"

I'm not ready to discuss my transition with all of our neighbors, so I change tracks quickly. "Why don't you tell Asher first?" I suggest. She agrees to call Jesse's seven-year-old son whom she's known her whole life. I catch snippets of their conversation.

"Do you know about my Mama? That she is changing and is going to be a boy?"

"Yeah. My dad told me."

"I don't like it. Don't you think she should stay the same?"

"I think if this is how he feels, he should do it, because he should be happy and will be a better dad. He is still the same person—he just might get a different body."

"I guess so. I just think he should stay the same."

"He will be a better dad if he gets to change! It might sometimes feel hard but you can talk to people who understand." Leigh's tone grows more gentle and relaxed throughout the conversation. When she gets off the phone, she is smiling and quickly runs back outside.

Later, and with less fanfare, I explain the same to three-year-old Ira: that Gail will be calling me "Nathan" and saying "he." My son doesn't say much, but later, as his mother tucks him into bed, he speaks up.

"I thought I would have a new name to call Mama."

"Well, if you want, you can call him 'Aba,'" Gail proposes, offering the Hebrew word for "Dad" to accompany her title of "Ima." So for several months afterwards, I'm both Mama and Aba to my kids. The pronouns and parental titles change depending on context, comfort and company. I don't demand a sudden switch, but do gently encourage a shift.

"Hey, I noticed that you called me 'Aba' a lot when we were at Jesse and Hannah's house last weekend," I tell Leigh one evening. "That felt really nice."

"Well, yeah, it's just easier there since they understand." She pauses before continuing. "Right now I call you 'Mama' or 'Aba' or 'Dad.' I think when it gets more inside, I'll just call you 'Aba' or 'Dad.' And after a while, once it's even more inside, then I'll just call you one of them. I wonder which one I will choose?" she continues, ruminating aloud. "I think it will be 'Aba.'"

"Well, do you think it's inside at all now, or not yet?" I ask.

"I don't think so," she replies pensively. "Actually, no, it is starting to be inside." She pauses again. "Actually, I'm just going to call you 'Aba' for the rest of the night." From that moment on, she's called me either Aba or Dad.

"Have you decided if you are going to change your body yet?" she inquires later that night.

"I think yes," I respond after sharing a meaningful glance with Gail.

"Are you going to right now?" she presses.

"No, it's going to be a while. It's not something I can do right away and it takes a long time," I say calmly.

"Oh, so are you going to do it when I'm a teenager?"

"No, I think sooner than that."

"Maybe when I'm seven or eight?"

"Yeah, probably more like that."

"I think you should talk to Jesse. Because he knows all about changing his body since he's done that and he's your friend. And if you talk to him, then maybe you won't feel scared because he can tell you all about it," she concludes thoughtfully and I think that the conversation has reached its end. But before I tuck her into bed she resumes.

"It sure is a lot of work to change. I think that would be a hard thing to do. I'm glad I was born with a girl body. Because if I felt like how I do inside, but I was born with a boy body, I think I would want to change." That's when I know she's completely on board with my transition.

As Leigh starts relaxing into our new family form, I stop worrying that I'm hurting her. Instead, I see how we can grow closer and that, by living in our family, she's learning more deeply about honesty, bravery and love.

At the same time, she helps me grow: knowing I must answer to a six year old with the uncanny ability to ferret out the truth helps me find the strength to move forward. My daughter is a quick and thorough thinker. She is vocal about her opinions and thoughts, and demands absolute clarity from the adults around her. I know I owe it to her to be clear about who I am—inside myself, in our family and as her parent.

Ira, on the other hand, is more of a mystery. He seems to roll with the punches but one afternoon he runs by, stops and looks me dead in the eye.

"Mama, I wish you would stay a girl," he announces before racing off.

Later that night, I get him all snuggled up and ask if he wants to talk some more. He nods.

"I'm sad. I think you should stay the same," he says quietly.

"I'm the same person inside," I reply. I go on to remind him how I'll always be his parent, that he'll always be my kid and that I'll always love him. He listens silently.

I know in my head that it won't help him, or anyone in our family, for me to just go backwards, to somehow un-know. Nonetheless, it's excruciating to hear him say "please don't change."

But as with Leigh, his most clearly stated struggle comes just before a deeper comfort. After that night, he starts calling me "Aba" consistently. Since then, he's developed a strong identification with me as his father, clearly looking to me as he discovers his own gender identity. In some ways we've traveled a similar course, both joyfully realizing what it means for us to be male.

Much of my life is still in flux, but my place in my family as Aba, as a dad, is solid. Parenting is where I first saw the kind of man I could be, the kind of man I am.

Each time I've taken a step forward, with my family beside me, I've had to form clear answers to direct questions from my children, to feign calm when I didn't feel it—until eventually, I actually felt it. I've asked a lot of my kids, but I also believe these particular children are in our particular family for a reason: they wouldn't be here, with us, unless they could do this.

PATRICK, PAT AND MEL

Chad Ratner

By age twenty-seven I'd already worked as a Spanish teacher, a mortgage loan funder, a Notary Public and a coffee shop supervisor—I guess I was trying to find my niche. The latter felt like a good place to land at the time, mostly because I was able to build several strong friendships there. My coworker Patrick, who became my unofficial mentor, was one of the few people in my life with whom I truly felt comfortable. Something about his honesty and sensitivity always helped me identify with him; he openly shared stories of being a DJ and former record executive as well as a former addict. Like me, he was adopted as a child and openly bisexual.

At work, Patrick was always encouraging me and pushing me to be better. From him I learned how to handle difficult customers and challenging situations. He led by example and inspired me, whether it was making the perfect cappuccino or remaining calm under pressure. As time passed, our friendship grew.

One day, years into knowing Patrick, I'd gone to visit my parents at their house. My mother, father and I had sat down at the kitchen table and I'd explained how I was struggling to pay rent after the mortgage industry collapsed, eliminating my part-time Notary income. As I was getting ready to leave, my father had held a one hundred dollar bill in front of me. But as I reached to take the money, he'd snatched it away.

"From now on at work, keep your head down, your mouth shut, and be a good girl," he'd said, as if I were his employee. He'd always been a controlling CEO who thought he could buy whatever he wanted. Insulted, and imagining how it would feel to punch him in the face, I nonetheless grabbed the bill and left without a word.

Later that day, Patrick came over to my apartment to find me fuming about what my father had done. As I finally verbalized my feelings, I tried to grasp how he could have said what he did. *Had I been his son, would he have still told me to keep my mouth shut and my head down?* I knew from the way he behaved that, to the contrary, he would have encouraged me to be assertive.

Patrick understood completely; I think he knew, long before I did, that I was struggling with something deeper.

"I feel more like a son than a daughter," I mentioned partway through our conversation. "I want to be treated that way."

"I've always seen you as a male," he responded casually. Shocked and embarrassed, I immediately felt the room start to spin. I felt sick. *He knows that I secretly feel male. What do I do?*

"I don't want to have any more problems in my life. Why do I have to have another problem?" I answered, starting to cry.

"You don't have a problem. There's nothing wrong with you," he replied. "You're just a dude born in the wrong body." As we discussed this, I became more and more stunned—he had *several* friends who he referred to as "transgender" or "transsexual." And he embraced that I might be, too, without judgment.

"Look online for information and support groups," he suggested. As soon as he left, I did just that. I didn't know exactly what I was looking for, but I was determined to find out more about transgender people.

It turned out he was right: there *was* a lot of information available. But I didn't know where to start or what to do with it, and much of it was negative. No one ever talked openly about this stuff and I had never met another transgender person. I had so many questions; alone and anxious, I needed someone to walk me through what this meant.

Eventually I came across the term "female-to-male" and started reading about women who transitioned to become men. I was amazed— I hadn't realized that this option existed! It sounded exactly like what I was going through.

Luckily, after striking the right combination of words in a Google search, I found an email address for a guy named Pat who was the head of a female-to-male support group at The Center Orange County. I sent him an email that night; it must have sounded desperate because the next day he replied with words of comfort. "First of all, take a deep breath. You are not alone."

Pat went on to welcome me into his group, suggesting I join them for the next date and time. I was instantly relieved to find someone who had gone through the same thoughts and feelings I had. But when the day of the monthly "FTM" meeting arrived, I almost missed it. Talking with friends at the coffee shop, I suddenly realized I had somewhere important to be. I figured I could still make it if I left right away, even though I was terrified to go alone. Gathering all of my courage, I rushed out. "Late or not," I told myself as I ran, "I need whatever information I can glean from this meeting."

I arrived at the Center so nervous I was shaking and stood wide-eyed when I got to the designated room. A group of men sat in a circle talking. They paused and looked up as I explained I was looking for Pat.

"I think I might be in the wrong place," I added.

"I'm Pat," one of the men answered and invited me to sit down with them.

As I listened to the group discuss hormones and surgeries, it suddenly occurred me: *All of these men used to be women! Oh my God!* Glancing at Pat, I was struck by his facial hair and how he was balding— I never would have guessed he wasn't born male. *Wow! Could this be the answer I'd been searching for? Could I really become male and lead a regular life?*

Elated, I looked around the room at these average-looking men, listening to them discuss their jobs and families. By the end of the meeting I realized that I needed to transition as soon as possible by beginning testosterone therapy. Also, I learned that I could have surgeries too to make my appearance more masculine. But by far the most helpful part of the experience was seeing other people who had gone through the same struggles I had. I was no longer alone.

———

Even though beginning to physically transition greatly improved my life, I still had difficult days. Dating could be especially hard. People who knew me would say that I seemed confident, but I was simply a decent actor. I struggled with intimacy; even meeting people at bars was challenging.

If an attractive guy or girl hit on me, I didn't know how to react. I immediately felt like they wouldn't be interested anymore—or would even be disgusted—if they knew I was trans. And there was always the possibility of violence if "the wrong person" found out. I decided I had to deal with these difficult feelings; I had to do something positive.

I became very active as a signature gatherer for equal marriage, a public speaker, a regular contributor to our local LGBT magazine, a trans support group co-facilitator and a board member for my county's Transgender and Equality Coalitions. After years of hormone therapy and having had gender confirming surgery, I started making myself available to other people struggling with their gender as I once did. I reflected deeply on how feelings of isolation and depression could accompany being trans, primarily due to social stigma—and I couldn't stand the thought of other trans folks feeling inferior or abnormal just because the majority of society didn't understand them.

With thoughts like these in mind, I decided last year I would join the setup crew for a local Transgender Day of Remembrance. When the night arrived, it turned out to be cold and wet. I walked through the rain, stopping short when I spotted a woman setting up candles for the ceremony. *Those would look better in a different pattern*, I thought to myself.

As I walked over to rearrange them, the woman flashed me a look but let me continue. I already knew her name since we were Facebook friends: Mel. But this night was the first time I'd encountered her in person. I felt intimidated by her reputation as a well-known activist in the LGBT community, and now I was struck dumb by her beauty. *I have to get to know her better.*

The next day I began commenting on her Facebook updates. She flirted back and eventually gave me her phone number. I thought she knew I was transgender, but she didn't until I came out to her via text message. After that evening, I couldn't help but wonder if her feelings towards me would change.

———

One night Mel and I were texting back and forth while she was laid up with a sprained ankle. Eventually, she invited me to her house.

"I'm on pain medicine for my injury and probably won't have the courage to ask you any other time. . ." she said eventually. "Do you want to come over?" I definitely did, and soon enough I found myself reading her address.

"But don't dress up or shower because I'm sitting around in sweatpants! It wouldn't be fair if you looked better than me," she added. I swore I wouldn't and jumped in my car. When I arrived we sat on her couch and nervously watched TV for hours.

When we talked, I found her intelligent and quick-witted—not to mention pretty. Moreover, we shared similar passions. Mel had volunteered with the Democratic Party and also worked towards marriage equality for same-sex couples. I was lucky she had offered to help with Trans Day of Remembrance that year or I never would have met her.

As we chatted, my heart pounded faster. When I realized it was getting late, I decided to make my move. "Well, if I'm gonna kiss you, I might as well do it now," I said and leaned over, my palms sweaty and my head spinning from taking such an uncharacteristic risk.

To my surprise, she kissed me back. I can only describe the moment as magical. But after we'd kissed for a while, she stopped. "You should go home. I need to process things," she said.

I must have passed her processing test because after that night, we became inseparable. I always suspected that if I had a chance to meet the right person, it would be through community work we shared.

Together, Mel and I phone banked for equal rights, went canvassing door to door and became even more involved in the LGBT movement. During a protest of an anti-LGBT organization at Disneyland, I fell in love. Looking at her in a Cinderella dress, holding a marriage equality sign and waving at cars, I knew I'd found the one.

I began saving up for a ring right away. A year into our relationship, I took her to her favorite place—Angel's Stadium—and asked her to be my wife. We were married the next summer.

A few months later we decided to vacation in Maui with my family. As I swam in the open ocean with sea turtles, I reveled in being shirtless and being able to have a beautiful woman snorkeling beside me. I felt lucky to be with my parents and sisters, who had stuck by my side throughout my transition. Today, Mel and I are in the process of starting our own family by adopting a child. My life couldn't be any better and I wouldn't change a thing.

BIG SHOES TO FILL

Gus

I grew up wearing my dad's shoes and hats around our busy house, knowing one day I wanted to be a father just like him. Fortunately, life provided me a son. Joseph was hell-on-wheels at eighteen-months-old when I met his mother; by that time, his biological father was long gone and I was five years into transitioning. Nearly every medical step was behind me, save lower surgery.

With dark wavy hair and big brown eyes, Joseph looked just like me. Strangers have always assumed he was biologically mine, which immediately helped me feel connected to him. However, he didn't call me "dad" right away; I wouldn't have let him even if he had. Fatherhood is too often taken for granted. So many men help conceive children and then contribute little or nothing to the people they become. No, I couldn't just walk into a child's life and overnight and be his "dad." So, he called me by my first name for two years.

Then one day when I was picking him up from daycare, it just *happened*. Sitting with his little friends, his face lit up as soon as he saw me.

"That's my dad!" he exclaimed, pointing me out to the other children. "He is a mechanic. He can fix *anything*!"

That moment changed me: I felt I'd absolutely earned the title. I knew now that Joseph was as proud of me as I was him. He *chose* me and I *chose* him. We made a tacit commitment to each other independent of my relationship with his mother. This proved vital, as she and

107

I never achieved a truly healthy partnership. We fought constantly, she was dishonest and I knew my friends and family disapproved. As much as I hated to admit it at the time, I couldn't blame them.

After a couple of years of chaos I knew I no longer loved her, but I adored Joseph. What's more, I felt he needed me; leaving him would be like cutting out the necessary, joyful half of my heart to spite the necrotic one. So his mother and I remained together for three more years.

Then one weekend I took Joseph to visit family members a couple of hours away. When I called to tell her we were on our way back home, she was acting strange and almost whispering. "What's going on?" I asked, becoming suspicious. In response, she told me she had been seeing someone else. She wouldn't be at the house when we returned.

Joseph stayed with me for about a month after that, but once he finished up the school year she came and took him. For almost a year afterwards, he was kept from me.

—•—

I can't begin to explain the anguish I endured in my son's absence. Though I was relieved my relationship with his mother was over, I was heartbroken that he'd been ripped away. She had promised she would never do that, but somehow I wasn't surprised; part of me knew that's why I stayed as long as I did.

Still, I couldn't help being bitter. I wanted to lash out and make her feel exactly what I'd tolerated to be in his life. But I knew if I did, there would never be a chance of her reconsidering. So I internalized my grief and spent a lost year writing Joseph a mountain of letters about how much I missed him and what was filling my days without him. I kept his room exactly the way he'd left it.

At the same time, life moved on. I met and started dating Kelly, the woman who would become my wife. I gradually let myself become attached to her son Michael. They eventually moved in with me. And though I was overjoyed by my new beginning, nothing was able to fill the emptiness Joseph had left.

In the end, it turned out to be best for him that I managed to hold my tongue. Inevitably, chaos erupted in my ex's life and she asked me to take our son. He's lived contentedly with me, Kelly and Michael ever since. He and his stepbrother were even able to be a part of planning our wedding. Both proudly walked down the aisle as ring bearers. Today, it feels perfectly natural to have two active boys in the same home I grew up in.

Neither Joseph, who's now nine, nor Michael, who's four, knows that I'm a trans man. Kelly and I decided to wait until the boys are older and mature enough to grasp that my road to manhood looked profoundly different than theirs will. I'm not sure that either of them would understand, at this point, what transitioning *means*. Neither boy was around to see me prior to the changes in my voice, face and body brought about by years on testosterone; had they been, explaining would probably have been unavoidable. As it stands, my trans history doesn't have much to do with how I parent day-to-day.

My approach comes almost entirely from my dad's playbook—in other words, it has nothing to do with my transition. Parenting is about the needs of dependent little people. They need love, nourishment, shelter; to learn how to share and to be kind and thoughtful. I have a strong desire for my own sons to have childhoods that are as carefree as possible. I hate that I was aware of how cruel the world can be as a child. I don't want my boys to be burdened with similar feelings of shame lurking under the surface.

But it would be dishonest to say I possess everything I'll ever need as a father. I wish I had more time—time that I didn't have to spend worrying about teachers or other kids' parents figuring out that Joseph's dad and Michael's step-dad wasn't always a man. Time unconsumed by worrying that they'll be treated unfairly because I'm in their life.

Kelly, on the other hand, is more concerned with the future. She wants to wait until they're both well beyond their rebellious teenage years. She fears how it would hurt me if they lashed out in anger at me being trans, even if the rage was ultimately about something else.

In the end, I don't really know when I'll tell them. Joseph knows I'm not his biological father, so I haven't been dishonest. I wouldn't ever want Michael's father to know for fear of him using it against Kelly to obtain custody. I'm hoping I'll sense when the time is right to disclose. When that moment arrives, I hope that both boys will love and respect me enough that it won't affect our relationships. And I hope that they'll recognize how being a dad was one of the single most important goals in my life. Perhaps most importantly, I hope that I'll have passed on the valuable lessons my dad instilled in me.

———

Life has gone in a circle: I followed my father around and tried to be just like him as a child and I find myself acting just like him as an adult. I was always a masculine kid who, much to my mother's disliking, never had girly toys or clothing forced on me. My dad didn't want my "spirit broken"; he believed I should be allowed to naturally outgrow my tomboy ways. So I climbed trees, carried a pocketknife, got into fights with other boys and even played in a male football league.

Granted, that last one took some convincing. My cousin Devin was a benchwarmer on a local team; his father, my uncle-in-law Jim, was one of those parents who gets kicked out of games nowadays for disruptive antics. It was his suggestion that I join. Looking back, he was probably using me to motivate his son to try harder by shaming him with a female cousin for a teammate. Devin and I were close but slightly competitive, having been born only five months apart.

"No!" was Dad's emphatic response to Uncle Jim's suggestion that I accompany him to the team's next practice.

"I don't see why not, she already knows how to play. The team could really use some more players. And it's not like she'd get hurt! If anything, we'd have to worry about the boys!" Jim replied. Dad laughed but remained firm.

"I don't think so. They don't allow girls to play."

"Hell, everybody always thinks she's a boy! Just let them think it." Jim was reading my mind. Dad hesitated for a fraction of a second. It was all the opportunity I needed to squeeze into the discussion.

"Please, Dad? I know I'll be good at it! We could cut my hair—" but he headed me off before I could finish.

"You're not getting a flat top haircut! We've already discussed that and the answer was *no!*" he said, recalling my failed attempt to convince him I should have a trim like my little brother's while school was out for summer. I took a calculated risk and insisted.

"No, it wouldn't have to be a flat top. Just a little shorter would be perfect!" He heard me out, but shelved the conversation until he had a chance to think about it. Meanwhile, Mom refused to take me for a haircut in protest at the idea of it all.

A week later Dad sat me on the picnic table in the backyard. When he hesitated momentarily, I started to worry that he'd second-guess his decision. But he kept the scissors in his hand.

"You sure you want to do this?" he asked one last time. I nodded silently and beamed. As Dad worked, the wind blew clippings into my mouth and I felt a small weight—more than just hair—falling from my shoulders.

I can recall that haircut more vividly than my first practice or game. For the rest of the season, I went by my initials and used male pronouns. I had a pretty exceptional childhood, but hearing others refer to me as "he" was one of the absolute highlights. It just felt right.

Then puberty came along and placed that weight—and then some—back on my shoulders.

———

My adolescent body betrayed me in ways I wasn't prepared for, and it made me absolutely miserable. I stopped walking tall and proud the way Dad did; instead I slouched to hide my forming breasts. And the worst part was that I didn't know how to talk to him about what was making me so incredibly unhappy.

At the same time, I knew my parents were hoping I would outgrow being a tomboy. I hadn't been blind to Mom's disapproving looks and I'd overheard discussions that turned into arguments, usually ending with Dad trying to reassure her that my masculinity was a phase. But it wasn't happening fast enough for her.

One of my first birthdays as a teenager, my kitchen filled up with a group of mostly male cousins and a couple of neighborhood boys I liked to pal around with. The date always fell right before the beginning of the school year, so I was used to receiving new school clothes.

As Mom handed me a familiarly shaped clothing gift box, I had no reason to be suspicious. I tore it open heedlessly and stopped short: *training bras*. I wanted to melt away. My face was on fire and the sound of my cousins and friends laughing sounded muffled, like my head was underwater. I could hear my pulse in my ears.

I could tell Dad hadn't known that Mom had planned to have me unwrap the bras in front of everyone. He was as red-faced as I was. But what I *couldn't* gauge was whether it was out of embarrassment for me or fury towards my mother. Later, I listened to my parents talking in low voices.

"You shouldn't have humiliated her in front of people," he admonished. But Dad had chosen not to override her authority in front of my brother and me.

So a couple of nights later, perhaps reassured in knowing my father would back her up, she told him of how I'd refused to wear the bras. He turned to me.

"Young lady, you *will* start wearing them if I have to take you in there and put them on you myself! Do I make myself clear?" my father said in his low, serious tone as we sat around the dinner table.

I don't remember answering. I don't remember the first time I put on one. All I *do* remember is that I was never without one after that. To my mind, the only thing more horrific than having to wear the darn things was the idea of my Dad putting one on me.

———

I had just started attending college two hours from home when I discovered transition was possible. A friend moved away and left behind a letter announcing his intention to become a man. For the first time I felt that there was someone in the world who understood me. I had so many questions about how to do it, but had no doubt that transition was the only answer for me.

The only thing I feared was losing my family. Mom was from a large town and seemed somewhat accepting of people's differences. Dad, on the other hand, was aging and set in his ways; he had been forty-five when he became a father. Born into a rural Southern town, he'd always been staunchly opinionated and conservative. So my worries began centering on him as I tried to get up the nerve to start the conversation. I just couldn't imagine him wanting to understand, let alone supporting me through my changing gender.

In retrospect, I'm not sure why I underestimated him. Perhaps it was because his disapproval would've been the most disappointing. Perhaps I was simply preparing for the worst. Whatever it was, I anxiously practiced what I might say in my truck on the way to our house, but the drive wasn't long enough for me to pick anything satisfactory.

When I arrived, I made awkward small talk before finally spitting it out. I can't even remember how I ended up saying it, oddly enough. But I can clearly recall Dad's worried look as he sat there and tried to absorb what I was saying.

After that, our initial conversations were clumsy and cautious. He struggled to articulate questions; when he managed to, they were vague inquiries about whether testosterone would have dangerous risks or the safety and success rates of surgeries. He wasn't a man who asked many questions, let alone really graphic or personal ones. So it sometimes took him months to get around to saying what was on his mind. I think a lot of his struggle lay in being unable to envision how I'd ever look or live in the world as a man, at least before seeing it with his own eyes.

He clearly also grappled with the thought of me not having a penis. "Will you have *functional business* after surgery?" he asked one day.

At the time, lower surgery seemed unimportant compared to the basic changes that would help me pass as male: a low voice, facial hair, not needing to bind my breasts and having my name and gender markers changed on legal documents. I had immediately sought testosterone;

my chest reconstruction and full hysterectomy followed about a year later. So when Dad asked me if I'd have a "working" penis, I told him it wasn't that important to me.

"Why would you go to all that trouble and not go the whole way?" he replied, bewildered.

"I don't know. It's expensive and—"

"—I don't think that would be the thing to stop me, if it were me that wanted to be a man," he cut in. "How does one see himself as a man if they don't want the thing that a lot of the world measures a man by? I know they say that size isn't everything, but not having one at all? What kind of women will you date? How will you explain not having a penis to a woman? What will you do in the men's room? Don't get me wrong, I hate to see you go under the knife at all. But I don't see you being satisfied just going part way with this."

Little did I know how right Dad would be. Gradually I realized I wouldn't be fully satisfied without genital reconstruction. I just wasn't able to think that far ahead because of the other milestones that concerned me at the time. It's amazing how much wisdom and insight he had even when he still wasn't sure about the idea of my transition.

———

I understand now, as a father, how parents grieve when they're letting go of hopes for what their child's life will look like. But as a young adult, all I saw was my own need to live for myself. Many times when my parents would struggle with pronouns or slip and use the old name, I'd get pretty impatient about correcting them.

"This is a lot to ask of me and your dad!" Mom would reply angrily. Dad, though, would just rub his eyebrows and sigh.

"Dang it! I'm sorry. Old habits die hard. I'm trying."

Once I'd been on testosterone for a year, I noticed him becoming much more consistent with the male pronouns. After another year, he started calling me "buddy" and "son" and talking to me in the same man-to-man fashion he'd always used with my younger brother. He'd joke about women, explain his views on men's etiquette and give advice on getting by in the kinds of blue collar work environments we both labored in. He offered encouragement when he sensed I needed it. He also delivered some harsh truths.

My initial two years on testosterone, I grew out my facial hair every few months before shaving, hoping to see it fill in. The first time I thought that I *might* have enough for a goatee, Dad took one look at me and had to comment.

"Son, don't take this to heart, but I think you need to think back to when your brother grew his first beard. You were pretty rough on him about it. He was excited and thought it looked better than it did. I hate to tell you, but that's about what yours looks like right now," he said, slapping me on the back. "Give it time." As he walked on, I resolved to shave and try again in a few months.

Five years later, he was diagnosed with cancer. Over time, he'd come to genuinely treat me as his second son. He'd given me day-to-day manly advice, listened to my petty troubles with jobs and women and coached me on ways to be a more patient dad to Joseph. But suddenly, knowing our time was ticking away, he and I started having even more meaningful conversations.

"Son, I hope I've taught you everything you need to know. I wish I'd known when you were little. Maybe we could've dealt with this sooner," he remarked one afternoon while we were riding around in his old pickup.

"Dad, I didn't know how to talk about it. I didn't know there was anything that could be done about it. How could you know if I couldn't tell you?"

"Well, I always wanted you and your brother to be able to talk to me about anything. Your brother . . . I guess I treated him differently. I loved you both the same. It was easier when you were little. You followed me everywhere. Then things changed and you just shut off. I didn't know what was going on," he answered sadly.

"I'm sorry, Dad. I didn't either. I know it wasn't what you would've chosen for me—I just hope I haven't been an embarrassment. I hope you've never felt ashamed of me," I replied, laying out my deepest misgivings so he would know I never wanted my transition to hurt him or Mom.

He shook his head and placed a hand on my arm. "Now why would you be an embarrassment? You work hard. You have a level head on your shoulders. You took an unusual road to get there, but you're a good man. You act the way I'd expect my oldest boy to act. I feel like you've got a lot of me in you. I'm proud of you. I just wish your brother would straighten up and be more like you."

With those words, the last of my burdensome guilt and shame faded away. It was the only approval I'd ever need; no one has ever held as much weight in my eyes as he did and probably never will.

He's been gone for almost five years now, but I think about him all the time. I ask myself daily if I'm living in a way he could be proud of. When I lose patience with Joseph or Michael, I think of how he handled my brother and me in similar moments.

My father was many of the things that I am today: a good son, a devoted brother, a favorite uncle, a loving husband and a dutiful dad. Like him, I'm a tradesman and all-around handyman. I don't wear a trans history for the rest of the world: my identity is centered around the ways I'm like him. I'm a man, plain and simple. And I know a significant part of that is striving to take on the many other roles he had—the ones I haven't grown into yet—and hopefully someday filling the big shoes he left behind.

STANDING ON THE PRECIPICE

Emmett Troxel

I'm standing on the precipice of a cliff, looking down into a deep chasm. I take one look behind me and see a blackness even darker than what is before me. If I step forward, I may be carried by the wind to great heights or fall to my death. Either way, I can never go back. My stomach is churning and I am as joyous and exhilarated as I am frightened. I close my eyes and leap.

———

My first testosterone injection was a silent, private occasion. I sat on the edge of my bed, watching my cat stare up at me as I pushed a syringe full of oil and magic into my thigh. I had never felt so proud of myself, yet so petrified about not knowing what would come next.

That initial moment of self-actualization seemed a long way off from where I had started. Though I had dreamt of it almost my entire life, I'd had to keep it a secret for decades, only admitting it to myself in the deepest recesses of my mind.

I'd been born to two very conservative parents in the suburb of a Midwestern city; I was sent to a private Christian school and gender roles were firmly enforced. We attended church multiple times a week.

In one of my earliest memories, I can recall helping my Dad with yard work. It was a particularly hot day, so he was mowing the lawn shirtless. At three-years-old, all I wanted to be was a good little helper, so I threw off my own top and ran outside to join him. But before I could get halfway down the deck stairs, my mother snatched me up mid-leap.

"You can't go outside with your shirt off!" she declared sternly.

"But I was just being like Daddy," I yelled back, surprised and ashamed.

"Well, he's a boy. He's allowed," she replied matter-of-factly.

Before then it had never occurred to me that girls had to act differently than boys—or that I *was* a girl, for that matter.

When I began attending school in the first grade, my favorite part of the day was coming home and trading in my girl shackles—the required long skirt or dress—for shorts and a t-shirt. I always felt out-of-place adhering to the institution's strict dress code, but I didn't try to rearrange my hair or ask my mom for fashionable outfits like the other girls. The one time my mother tried to put makeup on me—stage blush and eye shadow for a fifth grade play—I fought her the whole time.

"Mom, I hate this, why do I have to put on makeup?" I cried, tears streaming down my face as she reapplied mascara for the fourth time.

"Why are you fighting me? I don't understand why this is so hard," she replied. I rode all the way to school with my arms folded across my chest. When I got out of the car, a group of classmates stared at me.

"You look like a clown!" a girl exclaimed and everyone laughed. I put my head down and quietly walked to the back of the stage. As soon as my performance was over, I washed the makeup off.

As time went on, I felt more and more uncomfortable with being female. I started puberty around age eleven, a bit earlier than my peers. When I developed a chest, I hid it by crossing my arms and walking with my head lowered. I abhorred shaving my legs, putting on hose and shopping for bras. My first period was especially humiliating. I took one look at my stained underwear and threw it away; I didn't want anyone to know what was happening to me. My hair went from being stick straight to curly, so I was allowed to cut it short: my only relief.

When I was twelve, my mother came out as a lesbian and shortly thereafter my parents divorced. I began living part-time with each one and
attending public school. Because my new school didn't have a strict
gender-based dress code, I never wore a dress again. After my mother
came out, she was a bit more relaxed about my attire and didn't protest
when I started wearing boy's clothing and got my first buzz cut. I felt
more like myself.

A year later, I discovered I was attracted to women and announced
I was a lesbian at school. My first coming out was disastrous. I was spit
upon, teased and chased by my adolescent classmates. The parents of
the girl I had a crush on went to the principal and asked that I be sus-
pended because their daughter was so distressed. Later, a teacher sat
me down.

"You should be quiet about the whole 'gay thing' for your own sake,"
she suggested with contrived kindness.

But my father's reaction was the worst of all.

"I'm a lesbian," I told him as he was driving me home from school
one afternoon. His body stiffened, he sighed loudly and started driving
faster. I thought he was going to run the car off of the road.

"You're not homosexual, your mother is influencing you," he finally
growled. We sat in silence the rest of the way.

When we arrived, he followed me to my room. As I sat down on my
bed, he silently glared at me, gritting his teeth and flaring his nostrils. I
started crying.

"Why won't you accept me?" I sobbed.

"You can change this. You aren't really like this; you don't know
what you're talking about. Homosexuals are sick. You're sick. You need
to pray for God's forgiveness," he shot back.

"I can't control my feelings. When you have an erection looking at
a woman, you can't control it, can you?" I asked, using all the sarcasm I
could muster. He looked at me in shock, turned around and stormed out
of the room, slamming the door behind him.

I lived full time with my mother after that.

Late one night, I was looking through my mother's bookshelves, which were packed with all the LGBT literature a gay teenager could want. I picked out a book about a female-to-male transgender man who lived long before I was born and tore through it in one sitting. For some reason the story clicked and, though I was unsure how it related to me, I now knew it was possible to live as a man.

Two years later, I met my first girlfriend at a gay youth group. We hit it off right away and spent almost all of our time together. She became the first person with whom I had a sexual relationship. Curiously, I experienced a consistent fantasy that I would spontaneously grow a penis during sex. We role played scenarios where I was male so I could explore my feelings more fully. In that headspace, I felt complete and normal.

As time went on, I found my desire developing from a fantasy to a real need. When I told my girlfriend about how I longed to be a man, she was completely understanding. "You should do what makes you happy," she said.

"You're so brave," my close friends responded when I told them at the youth group a few days later. With newfound confidence and courage, I resolved to tell my mom I was transgender and that I wanted to start transitioning. I expected her, a feminist lesbian who had walked away from what she called a "religious paradigm," to be unquestioningly supportive. So I didn't see her reaction coming.

"I have a daughter, not a son. Don't hack off your body parts," she replied flatly.

"It was just a thought," was all I could stammer before I resumed silently emptying the dishwasher.

Her opinion mattered to me more than anyone's; she was the only authority figure to accept me as a lesbian. Her unexpected response evoked the fear and rejection that I had experienced from others, so in that moment I resolved to never transition. To cope, I built up a preposterous scenario in my mind that becoming a man would mean losing my family and any chance at a career. I believed I would inevitably end up homeless and unloved for the rest of my life.

For the next seventeen years, I lived as a trans man on the inside and a butch lesbian on the outside. I had other relationships with women throughout my teenage years, but never told them about my feelings. Then I met the woman who would become my wife at the same youth group where I met my first girlfriend. I was eighteen, and we've been together ever since. She's always accepted and supported me, and understood why I felt I couldn't transition. But my self-denial eventually took a toll.

I felt heavy-hearted and hopeless. I wasn't able to maintain relationships with friends because I could never share my true self. I couldn't relate to the women in my life because I knew I was not one of them. I couldn't relate to the men in my life because I was too jealous of them. Often I would stare in the mirror, repeating, "You're disgusting. What are you? You're not a woman. Look at you: you're a thing, a freak." I couldn't let my wife touch or look at me nude because my body felt wrong.

After fourteen years, she gently nudged me to start transitioning. "I can't stand your depression anymore. I want a partner, not a shell of a person," she told me one afternoon. At her urging, I started seeing a therapist who specialized in transgender clients.

My first appointment with him was crucial. He was the only person outside of my wife and ex-girlfriend who took it at face value that I wanted to be a man. I left a significant share of my pain and trepidation in the room that day. Though I was still unsure about my exact course-of-action, I knew that I was fundamentally okay—that whatever I decided was going to turn out for the best.

My second coming out proved much easier than the first. I began by sending my mother a lengthy email about my plan to transition. In it I explained how her initial reaction was one of the deciding factors behind hiding my feelings for years. When she called that night, I was completely surprised by her change of heart.

"I'm so sorry that my reaction caused you any pain," she managed through her tears.

We ended a meaningful conversation by agreeing to meet for lunch the next day at her house. For a few hours, we sat beside each other on her couch, earnestly discussing my intentions. She wept again and hugged me tightly with a heartfelt "I love you."

Since then our relationship has been closer than ever. We talk often and she even brags about her son to friends online. She joyfully sends me pictures of myself wearing boy's clothing as a child and has quietly stored the ones of me wearing dresses.

Coming out to my Dad was, on the other hand, a predictably negative experience. Over the years, we had tried to build a tenuous relationship. But when I told him I was trans in an email, he didn't respond for two weeks. Finally, I called him.

"I couldn't think of anything to say," he admitted nervously. So we decided to discuss it over lunch.

The next day we met at a cheap Mexican restaurant and sat across the table staring at each other blankly for most of our meal. He gave me the same off-putting look he had eighteen years earlier: teeth gritted, nostrils flared. Again he blamed transition on my mother, though this time because she had "bisexuality in her family."

"Can you call me by my new name?" I asked after an hour of strained conversation.

"Maybe one day I will consider it," he said, glaring at me, then looking off into the distance. Later he added, "You are my daughter, even if you don't think you are."

Eventually, we both got angry with each other and I decided to leave. "I'm glad we had this talk, I know how you feel now," I said as I stood and, after a quick half-hearted hug, I walked away without cleaning up my mess. After all I'd put up with, I figured he could deal with my trash.

I'm not sure what it is about my gender that my father is so attached to, but I've decided that it's his problem, not mine. Still, if he ever comes to me with a genuine gesture of support, I'll welcome him. Until then, it's not worth the heartache to continue our relationship.

Looking back, if I had somehow known that only one person would reject me, I would have transitioned sooner. Looking forward, I know I will not always walk an easy road. I face decisions about what type of surgery I want, the waiting game of adopting children, the fear of being outed to unfamiliar people. However, these all feel minor compared to the despair I experienced before I started my journey—before I closed my eyes and leapt off of the cliff.

Some mornings I wake up thinking "What have I done?", but as time goes on, those moments are becoming fewer and fewer. Every "sir" and every "he" increases my confidence; every hair on my face and every crack of my voice makes me smile. Inside of me, there has always been a little boy and finally he gets to grow up and become a man.

PART III

MEN LIKE ME

MEN LIKE ME

A. Scott Duane

I lay in his bed, legs drawn to my chest, desperate and helpless. I was disgusted and disgusting.

"What am I going to do?" I sobbed. "I can't leave the house like this."

Bruce shrugged dismissively. "We'll just go get you some Maxipads. No big deal."

At that moment, I hated him. My boyfriend. My partner. A recent trick had given him gonorrhea and he'd passed it onto me. Now my cunt was leaking uncontrollably. We had to go to the store, so I pulled myself together and dumped myself into his car, depressed and humiliated. On the way I told him, "I need bottom surgery."

I wasn't using "need" as a trite synonym for "want"—I meant that I yearned for a body that was different. I craved it. Food, water, shelter, penis.

Bruce shifted uncomfortably at my revelation. "Fine," he said. He loved my parts in that enviable, simple way that I wished I could love them too. "I just wonder why you'd want to give up something that brings you so much pleasure."

A year earlier, I was in Joel's living room. He'd made me a gaudy green skirt, and he was adorning it with sparkles and even gaudier green fabric for trim. We'd gotten the idea on a recent trip to Disneyland. Never a skirt-wearer growing up, I'd felt a sudden excitement at the idea of trying on a glittery fairy princess dress. He promised that when we returned, he'd make me a Tinker Bell outfit.

As he sewed, his phone rang. "I can't talk right now," he answered. "I'm making my boyfriend into a fairy."

Joel was a trans man like me, but seventeen years older and ten years further into transition. We were close for the first couple of years of my own transition, and boyfriends for a good portion of it. With him, I explored the world of gay men. Under the safe wings of a man just like me, I went to all-male BDSM events, gay men's sex clubs, leather bars. We weren't natives, but Joel taught me the language and the customs. Often, no one knew we were only naturalized citizens of gay male culture. We had the special bond of two visitors to a strange and foreign place.

Even when I wore a skirt, I was a man with Joel. There was no qualification, no doubt. With Joel, I discovered my sexuality as a queer man. And I embraced my own queer manhood, too.

Bruce came later. I brought with me my newly unabashed effeminacy, my fairy wings, my tutus, my queerness. And I had a cunt, too. For Bruce, it was a confusing combination. Despite my masculine physique, convincingly male voice and a respectable amount of facial hair, he called me "she" on our second date. Even though a little flare of warning shot up when he said it, I kept seeing him. There was so much else that I liked, and eventually loved, about him. I didn't want my sensitivity about my gender to get in the way of something good.

Over the months that we were together, the illusion that a relationship was always and automatically a safe haven in which I was sure to be seen and accepted as a gay man dissolved bit by bit. There was the time that a man at a party bore an inextricable resemblance to my friend Mark, another transguy. Bruce said, "He can't be trans. He's too male."

There was the time he told me another friend wasn't really serious about transition because he hadn't gotten together the money for top surgery yet and, as a result, didn't pass very well. There was the time he referred to himself as "the guy" in the relationship, and me as "the girl." And there were the fights that ensued after, when he'd usually tell me I wasn't giving him enough credit; after all, he saw me as a guy most of the time, he just slipped occasionally. Wasn't that enough?

With other people, "sometimes" could be enough. My parents still called me "she" almost all the time. Acquaintances would sometimes ask awkward and misinformed questions. It happened. But in a relationship, I couldn't be a part-time boyfriend, part-time girlfriend. I needed to be a boyfriend, without qualification, all the time. Months of being with a cis guy who made "small mistake" after "small mistake" broke me down in a way I couldn't have predicted.

When we broke up, I found myself thinking of Joel, and believing that only other trans men could really understand me. But as much as I loved my trans brothers, I was just so tired of feeling like a visitor among cisgender men.

After Bruce, I made two important decisions. First, I vowed to get bottom surgery as soon as possible. At the beginning of my transition, I was adamant that I'd never change my genitals. They were fun sexually, and I believed the surgeries available wouldn't add anything that was worth the money and time. And on top of the medical and sexual objections I had, I was so effeminate. If I was comfortable running around in a skirt, bottoming to gay men and didn't know the Rose Bowl from a bowl of roses, why would I need a penis? The only trans guys (in my view) who went for bottom surgery were straight, macho, sports-loving, button-front shirt-wearing manly men. Not me. But as I'd developed into my body and my sexuality, the need for a completely male body, penis and all, became alarmingly strong. No matter how loose my attachment to social gender constrictions, I had to find a way to fulfill that need.

The second decision I made was to find the men like me.

———

Where does a man go to find community? Sports teams? Beer festivals? Book clubs? The truth is, I've found friendship and fulfillment in all of these places, but this search was about something more than that. So instead, I went to naked all-men's yoga. I found the ad in a local gay paper. I emailed the instructor, Paul, and told him my situation. I asked if I would be welcome at his class, having not yet had genital surgery. He replied, "You are absolutely welcome here. I have not had a trans man in my class before, but if anyone has a problem with it, I will just refund their money and send them home."

Rats! I thought. *He's so nice. Now I can't chicken out!*

It took me weeks to work up the courage. I drove by the little yoga studio, tucked into an ally in the Midtown neighborhood of San Diego between a strip club and a consignment furniture store, two weeks in a row. When I'd get close, worst-case scenarios began playing in my head. A room full of naked men eyeing my odd body with disgust. Would they laugh? Would someone say with unbearable genuineness, "I thought this class was for men?"

Put on your big boy pants, Scott, I thought on the third week. *The worst won't happen. And if it does, you'll deal with it. Just leap.*

The instructor was already naked when I walked in, as were most of the other guys. A man smiled at me from his mat as he stretched. When I told him who I was, Paul said, "Yes, I remember. You're welcome to be nude, but if you want to keep your underwear on, that's fine too. However you're comfortable." Not having come so far to do this halfway, I got completely naked. I set up across from the man who had smiled so warmly. Now, he was unsure where to put his eyes. He wanted to look at me, but he wasn't sure what he was seeing. I relaxed into the knowledge that I wouldn't have to hear his voice for the entirety of the 90-minute class. I heard only Paul's voice, and experienced the newness of yoga in my body. I basked in my very presence there, naked and male.

At the end of the class, we all got dressed amidst relaxed chatter. The others were friendly and warm to me, said hello, and asked how I'd liked the class. They asked about my studies, what sports I did ("You've got runner's calves."), and how I found the class. It didn't occur to anyone to criticize my body or even ask about my obvious anatomical differences. As I left, the man who had been seated uncomfortably across from me said, "Good night. I hope to see you again."

Naked yoga became a weekly staple. They all know that I'm a naturalized citizen to their world, but we don't talk about it much. My genitals have only been a topic of conversation once, in fact, during the two weeks preceding my bottom surgery. I quietly let the instructor know that I wouldn't be back for a while because I'd be recovering. As we left the studio and walked into crisp forty-degree air, one of the guys slapped me jovially on the back and said, "The real test of whether your surgery is a success will be if your balls shoot up into your stomach in weather like this!"

It's just a yoga class, but for me, it was my first taste of brotherhood. I'm not just like the other men there. My body will always be a little different. The way I came to manhood is unique. Nonetheless, they've made a little spot for me in their circle. I've never felt like a visitor there.

———

As I approached bottom surgery, being with other men took on special significance. Genital transformation was the last step for me into the world of men, and it seemed fitting to be with them as I approached that step. The weekend before my metoidioplasty,[1] I ventured two hours north of San Francisco to the Billy Gathering, a weekend retreat for gay, queer and bisexual men. The Billys were mostly nature-loving older gay men. Many of them had never met a trans man before. Most didn't realize that I was trans until one of our morning heart circles—a daily ritual in which any man could share his thoughts and feelings on any subject.

The revelations in the heart circle were serious, incredibly emotional and sometimes heartbreaking. Perhaps a dozen men shared their loneliness and their inability to connect with other men. Others discussed their struggle with the expectation that they keep their feelings buried, that they stay silent instead of expressing their joy, fear, sadness and love.

Before speaking, I doubted that my share would be something that the others could relate to. First, I disclosed to the group that I was transsexual. I talked about my upcoming surgery, only two days away. I talked about the fear and uncertainty of not knowing what my body would be like afterward. I told them how excited and scared I was to complete my physical journey to manhood; after all, no one had taught me growing up what a man is supposed to be like. And certainly no one had showed me how to be a queer man. How would I know how to be in the world after this was all finished?

After the circle, the outpouring of support was overwhelming. The other men found my sentiments not only powerful and vulnerable, but exactly in line with their thoughts and feelings about being male. No one had showed them how to be queer men either.

It wasn't perfect. Sometimes people with the best intentions just don't have the right words. Many of them used the word "tranny" without knowing that it was a slur—and they used it in such a positive way! "San Francisco has so many trannies. I think you'll feel really supported here." And, of course, there was the barrage of questions after I disclosed in the circle: whether my family was accepting, what my name was before transition, what hormones I took, etc. I was in the spotlight and it wasn't totally comfortable.

But the negatives aren't what I remember. What has stuck with me is the man who told me, "So many of us here didn't have role models. And now we get to show you how men can be. What a privilege."

I had surgery two days later, full of optimism and hope. The objections and words of Bruce and all the others like him were, at that moment, inconsequential.

I haven't had my penis long enough to say how or if my new body part has changed my relationship to male culture. But I take a lot of comfort in knowing that I will be able to explore this new stage of transition among men like the naked yogis and the Billys—men like me.

NOT A CARICATURE OF MALE PRIVILEGE

Trystan Theosophus Cotten

> *I, as a Black woman, write with words that describe my reality, not with words that describe the reality of White scholars, for we write from different places. I write from the periphery, not from the centre. This is also the place from where I am theorizing, as I place my discourse within my own reality.*[1]
>
> —Grada Kilomba, *Plantation Memories*

Middle Passages

I almost froze to death inside a dumpster one night because I couldn't get a taxi to the house on Long Island where I was staying for the weekend. That evening I experienced an extended rendition of the black-man-can't-get-cab story that I'd heard often—a racial allegory illustrating black men's criminalization in the U.S. and its impact on our lives, down to the most mundane aspects of existence.

But usually this is where the tale ends: with the brother standing alone and dejected. The story doesn't go into what happens afterwards. Does the guy call a friend? Catch a bus instead? Start walking and get shot down by the cops who see nothing but a perp? Does he ever get to his destination? What happens to all the black and brown men who can't get cabs? I found myself pondering these questions while trying to stay warm and awake in sixteen-degree weather sitting in the midst of filthy garbage bags.

I'd spent the evening in Manhattan joyfully catching up with friends I hadn't seen in a while and caught a late train back to Huntington Beach. I arrived at the station around one o'clock in the morning to find three taxis waiting in the parking lot. Not one driver would accept me. When I walked up and tapped on their passenger side windows, each offered a different story of why he couldn't, or wouldn't, take me. Then, I watched incredulously as they accepted white customers who walked up after me.

The temperature was falling rapidly; I had to find shelter. Looking around, I spotted a lone police car parked off to the side of the train depot and momentarily considered asking for help, but then I remembered how awfully I'd been treated by cops since transitioning. I'd been racially profiled as a perp, thug, "illegal alien" and terrorist.

I recalled how I almost got shot in my own driveway by an Oakland cop who assumed I was a perp, when I was the one who'd called 9-1-1 to report a hit-and-run incident. When the cop arrived, he didn't ask any questions; instead, he drew his gun and demanded that I get down on the ground. If I hadn't complied, he may have shot me.

Lying there, I felt humiliated on so many levels. It felt like a surreal version of the 2009 debacle that Harvard professor, Henry Louis Gates, Jr., faced.[2] Malcolm X was right. Black men with PhDs are still niggers in a country and world controlled by whites.

I also recalled how cops had profiled me as an "illegal alien" and "Islamic terrorist" since transitioning. Less than a year earlier, I had been caught by surprise one afternoon when Emeryville police swooped in to surround me as I exited the post office. They came from all directions, including hovering from above in a helicopter. A security guard in a nearby building had been watching me on closed circuit camera and had called the police to report a "Muslim man" wearing a bomb vest and carrying packages into the post office.

Of course, the only thing I was guilty of was wearing a 40 lb. weight vest that I wear to maximize walking and running exercises. But on my light brown male body, it suddenly became a bomb! The cops demanded to know what I was carrying. Angered by their intrusion, I wanted to reverse the dynamic and make them feel some of my discomfort.

"It's a book on dicks. Transsexual men's dicks, to be more precise," I retorted. Their dumbfound facial expressions were priceless.

———

Ordeals like these have become daily occurrences since I transitioned. The time it's taken to accept my new reality has been compounded by memories of how I was treated very differently as a butch dyke. Although cops often clocked me as a black male from afar, my voice would eventually reveal my femaleness to them. Instantly, their attitudes, voices and tightened bodies would relax and become less threatening.

Embodying black manhood has helped me understand this ironic privilege. I had never considered the possibility that I had any *advantages* in this world as a masculine black female. Nor did I have a clue that I'd be in at least as much, if not *more*, danger in a male body. But masculinizing my body has taken away the option of performing femaleness at crucial times to ward off trouble, while also multiplying the various ways in which I am criminalized. As J. Halberstam has pointed out, a high-pitched voice can prove useful when entering women's pubic bathrooms, as a tool to allay occupants' fears that she's a man invading spaces designated for women.[3] Her "fluty" voice, and, I would add, the white skin that she doesn't mention, work together to legitimize her presence.

Not only am I lacking the female voice, smaller body and beardless face that once worked in my favor, but my brown skin imbricates my maleness to position me in the ranks of disposable bodies. What a supreme irony to discover that in liberating myself from the prison of my female body, I have become a target of the prison industrial complex.

My wife saved me from freezing to death on that fateful winter night at Huntington Station. With little power on my phone, I called her to leave a message explaining my predicament and letting her know how much I loved her. I knew that I couldn't stave off sleep much longer with the temperature dropping so rapidly and with my heart rate slowing, I'd eventually slip into a coma—the human body's natural biological response to freezing conditions. I didn't want to die without her knowing how I loved her. Then, I dozed off despite my best effort to remain alert.

Several hours later, my wife was awakened by "something" (she later said) that urged her to get up and check her voicemail. Her heart shattered with grief when she heard my voice. Immediately, she called 9-1-1 and spent over two hours on the phone trying to organize a search party from over three thousand miles away. Because my phone battery was low, she wasn't able to reach me and find out my location. Eventually, I was found by police around five a.m. I had never been so happy to see cops in my life!

Abandoning the Mistress' Tools

I am relatively new to black/brown manhood. I'm still learning how to navigate the world safely like my cisgender brothers, who've had the benefit of training since birth. They know how to deal with cops, how to navigate the world of men and women and how to cope with the insanity of living in a world made for white folks.

I have come to realize that if I'm going to survive, I have to learn the customs of this new social landscape and the ways that racism, Islamophobia and anti-migration inform it differently. I need a new language and coping strategies to help me survive the trigger-happy cops and white vigilantes.

All my years of reading, writing and teaching feminism didn't prepare me for the harsh materiality and corporeality of black and brown manhood.[4] The feminist tools I started my transition with are now inadequate for my survival and, depending on the circumstances, utterly disempowering. As I walk the new terrains of black male embodiment, I begin to critically question and, at times, abandon certain radical feminist ideas about straight men, male privilege and oppression.

A good example is the sexual harassment that I endured during my year-long tenure review process. A female student sexually harassed and stalked me for the entire year. Being sexually harassed by a woman blindsided me, because all my feminist training had indicated that only men could victimize women. My feminist classes and circles never discussed the possibility of the reverse.

Occasionally, someone would pose the theoretical possibility that women can oppress men, but we never explored what female oppression of men looks like. These questions were typically met with irritation and denial. We downplayed male victims as rare, explaining that women didn't have systemic power to become oppressors.

As months passed by without a foreseeable end to the stalking, I was unable to acknowledge, much less name, my oppression. My one-sided feminist perspective that men have all the power over women had deluded me into thinking that somehow I was in control of the situation, that I was responsible for my student's misbehavior. Ironically, my feminist training was leading me to dismiss my own feelings and intuitions in my new male embodiment. I found myself disempowered and even encouraged to collude in my own invisibility.

As I reached out to women and feminist colleagues for help, I was even more shocked by their lack of sympathy and support. My Department Chair (at the time) responded with laughter and dismissed the situation as a silly schoolgirl crush. Two more female colleagues gave similar responses of amusement, glossing over my need for support during the most stressful time of my career. I was up for tenure, yet couldn't get them to see the seriousness of the situation.

I was shocked at how callous they were to my predicament. I became angry when I considered the reverse situation. Had a male student been harassing me when I was female-bodied, people would have taken me more seriously and rushed to my rescue.

I changed my cellphone number twice, but the harassment continued. For the eight anxious months of my tenure review, the student stalked me by phone, email, Facebook and around campus. I agonized about being denied tenure and becoming unemployed—a shameful stigmatization that burdens many black and brown men psychologically.

My student only reacted with anger when I continued to enforce professional boundaries by reminding her of university policy concerning fraternization. As she became more petulant, I feared that she might retaliate against me by claiming that I had harassed her—or worse, that I had sexually assaulted her. It wouldn't be the first time that a man was falsely accused of harassing a woman.

My student could have said anything and it would have been difficult to disprove her allegations. The accusation alone would have been sufficient to smear my reputation beyond repair, regardless of substantial proof. Power imbalances of age, gender and institutional rank between us, combined with cultural constructions of black men and transsexuals as hypersexual deviants, would have made it impossible to defend my innocence.

I had many sleepless nights imagining media headlines: "Black Transsexual Professor Sexually Assaults Female Co-ed." The court of public opinion would have condemned me before a trial could even begin. The university probably would have settled out of court to avoid bad publicity, only reinforcing my guilt in the public eye. The scandal alone would have been enough to oust me from my position.

Eventually, I found a female colleague who truly listened and offered kind advice, but not until I had shared my ordeal with male colleagues and friends first. They validated my experience and shared their own problems of dealing with flirtatious female co-eds and co-workers.

These men genuinely considered my anxieties and suggested strategies that would have never occurred to me. Having dealt with such issues far longer than I, they advised me to save all the emails and texts just in case the situation escalated. They also encouraged me to report the student to the university attorney if the harassment continued and threaten to sue the institution for failing to protect me.

Listening to them, I came to realize how dysfunctional my response had been. I had blamed myself for not solving a problem that, in reality, I had no control over. Our conversations created a space for me not only to share my fears and frustrations, but also to name my own powerlessness. Together, our stories, fears and quandaries of sexual harassment had begun to complicate my feminist understanding of gender and sexual politics.

Before transitioning, it had never occurred to me that radical feminist views of men, gender and sexual politics could be inaccurate or fallible. While we critiqued patriarchal oppression, we failed to critically examine the limitations of our *own* social locations and embodiments. We simply assumed that men were always privileged and women were disadvantaged and defenseless. We never bothered to explore how men are also victimized by sexism. What is more, we assumed that our feminist analyses were correct and objective and whenever anyone challenged our views, we promptly branded them a misogynist.

Since transitioning, however, I have come to see that feminist analysis of men and male embodiment are just as limited and governed by political agendas as those of men writing about women. I now understand that many feminist understandings of men's lives aren't any more accurate or objective than men's views of women.

Men have voices and viewpoints about manhood and male culture that are valid and worth consideration. Transitioning has enabled me to open my ears to these multiple voices and pinpoint certain double standards in my own feminist politics.

Boxing and Barbershops

I've encountered camaraderie in places I least expected: the boxing gym, barbershop and street corners. The brotherhood I've found has been vital in my transition and survival. I had once considered these spaces incorrigibly sexist and homophobic. In my female/feminist embodiment I couldn't appreciate what these places mean for men and what men get from them socially, emotionally and spiritually: a brotherhood just as powerful as the sisterhood I found in women's communities.

Standing on the outside, armed with my radical/feminist/queer analyses, I pre-judged them as places that revel in misogyny and heteronormativity. For instance, boxing could only be understood as a display of hyper-masculinity and machoism, instead of a disciplinary practice instilling mental and physical toughness in men who have to navigate the absurd contradictions of black and brown

139

manhood. The barbershop, boxing gym and street corner are urban schools of black and brown male training where I'm learning how to survive and cope with the indignities of anti-black/brown racism. In these spaces I am not erased by some abstract concept of male privilege.

It's not that men don't have privilege. My problem is with the ways in which many feminists oversimplify mine and other (straight) men's lives, especially men of color, immigrant men, poor and working class men. Once I got past my truncated views of men, I saw how integral these spaces are to our survival—a powerfully humbling step in my transition journey.

When white feminists ask me about male privileges I've gained, I recount my stories of harassment and struggle and watch them frown in consternation. They grow quiet and seem uninterested in continuing the conversation. My stories don't fit into their theories, so these women have no interest in listening further.

A few might insist that I've gained male privilege on a structural level. They argue that I'm in a gender group that makes 25% more money than women and that the patriarchal system protects me over women. Yet, I have to remind them of how the university failed to protect me against sexual harassment and how the prison industrial complex uses their (cisgender) white womanhood as an excuse to harass and incarcerate black and brown men.

What is more, I am underpaid for my professional experience. Women fresh out of graduate school are hired at salaries higher than mine. Thus, the notion that I am protected and privileged by patriarchal institutions is spurious and dismissive of *my* corporeality as a black (trans) man.

———

When I joined the gym initially, I expected to hear a deluge of sexual conquest stories and relentless denigration of women. The radical feminist and queer theory and politics that I'd studied and lived by for nearly two decades portrayed straight men as sexist homophobes who benefited from women and gay oppression. But I haven't encountered a man resembling that caricature of hetero-sexual masculinity.

Instead, I've been pleasantly surprised to find so many compassionate and emotionally sensitive men who love, respect and protect women. When we rap about our problems with our jobs, kids, bills, relationships, aging, etc., there's a nurturing, brotherly quality to our conversations—a loving toughness or tough lovingness. In these private gatherings, men let their guards down and talk openly about their feelings, worries, hopes, yearnings and heartaches.

I enjoy boxing and mixed martial arts because they are rigorous, demanding and build character. Workouts are grueling and designed to enhance not only the body, but the mind as well. I listen and learn a lot from my brothers. Physical conditioning strengthens morale, resolve and tactical knowledge so I can fight effectively inside the ring. I listen and learn from my brothers so I can respond strategically and composedly to offensive forces.

I'm learning how to effectively deal with the trials and tribulations of being under- or unemployed, profiled by cops and hunted by vigilantes like George Zimmerman within a system that takes money from schools to build prisons.[5] Sparring teaches me how to stay focused—eyes on the prize—in the midst of chaos and to be more observant of minute details about people and my surroundings.

I am healing the emotional drinking and eating that crept up on me a couple of years into transition while trying to cope with the stresses of black and brown manhood. I was headed down the road of diabetes and hypertension that is so rampant in black and Latino communities. I hadn't expected to be under siege daily by cops. I had no idea what I'd gotten myself into with transitioning.

The brotherhood of boxing, however, pulled me from that wreckage and put me on a better path of self-love. Because the workouts and sparring are so demanding, I have learned to eat nutritiously to give my body what it needs to be effective. I rarely drink or smoke weed anymore. I feel much calmer now with an unflappable confidence that I am capable of handling any situation that arises.

The barbershop is another place where I experience soulful kinship with other black and brown men. Mac is the owner of the barbershop in San Francisco I frequent as much for the camaraderie as a haircut. After fighting three wars serving in both the Army and Navy, he's still standing tall and robust at the age of eighty-four. He's a rarity these days, a model of black male longevity.

Mac reminds me of the men in my family and 'hood when I was growing up. They were strong, gentle giants who worked from sunup to sundown at crappy jobs for scanty pay. They, along with our mothers, were our heroes—models of a black pride living in quietly dignified resolve.

Sometimes it's just Mac and me in the shop. Other times it's bustling with other guys talking and reading the paper. Some bring their kids. A precious sight that sticks in my memory is watching a guy get his hair cut while his two- or three-year-old child sits sleeping in his lap.

These men *love* their children. I see it in their proud, beaming faces when they talk about their kids or interact with them. They remind me of my own childhood when my mother's boyfriend used to take me down to the corner where he bonded with his buddies drinking cheap whiskey. These men bear no resemblance to the stereotypes of straight men as deadbeat dads that populated my feminist books and discussions.

Except on occasion, women don't enter the barbershop or boxing gym and thus aren't privy to the mentoring and bonding so essential to men's survival. These are places where we come together as men to commiserate, coach and confide in one another—a powerful nurturing experience. My daily grind as a black/brown man isn't dismissed here as man-griping or misogyny. Instead, I feel validated and mirrored by other guys. We testify and witness each other's struggles and longings.[6]

Mac is particularly wise, time-tested and still sharp. "Don't let 'em knock you off your game," he bellows in his authoritative baritone.

"That's what they want. That's how they get to you." He shakes his fist, "And if you let 'em get to you, then they win."

I learn lessons from him and my other brothers about how to stay alive in my new body and retain some dignity while being demeaned by the cops. I glean how to dodge potential danger and appear nonthreatening to women and white people. It's not a fail-safe toolkit against others' racist projections, but it's all I have to stay alive. None of us names this as *powerlessness*. Rather, we call it surviving a system that degrades and tries and tries to break down men of color, whether trans, cis or intersex.

The first lesson is being self-aware and cautious of my clothes, movements and facial expressions in public. I used to walk quickly and run to catch a bus. Now, I move at a slower pace and if I'm late I don't dare rush. I am hyper-aware of making sudden or abrupt movements, especially in airports, train stations and other public places like stadiums and parks. I never know who is watching and what assumptions they might make about my actions.

My buddies tell me to have eyes in the back of my head and be alert to where cops patrol. I avoid engaging with unfamiliar white folks, especially white women. I look away if they happen to look in my direction. If they catch my eye, white women usually clutch their purses and cross the street. They see me as a threat: a thug, rapist or terrorist. When I'm lost, I don't dare ask strangers for directions. I'll find my own way or ask a person of color. Women of color don't react to me fearfully, so I feel safer approaching them for directions.

While I love urban aesthetics, I stopped wearing hoodies and traded my baggy jeans, oversized jerseys and colorful skull caps for close-fitting jeans, khakis and sweaters. I replaced my high-tops with sandals, finger-shoes and dress shoes. These changes blunt assumptions that I'm going to snatch purses or merchandise, or jump the subway turnstile. The less visible I am, the less attention I draw to myself, the better are my chances of surviving.

I still, however, got pulled over frequently for Driving While Black more times in the last five years than the previous twenty years in a female body. Every time, without fail, I get the same hostile treatment and negative assumptions. The first two questions they always ask are:

"Do you have drugs or alcohol in the car?" and "Are you on parole or probation?"

While I didn't think twice about protesting prior to transitioning, I don't dare speak back anymore for fear of provoking them. I know that it doesn't take much now. My buddies have taught me that it's better to be calm and agreeable with the police. "You are not going to win that battle," says Mac, who still gets profiled at his age.

Lastly, my brothers have taught me that while my survival depends on taking racism seriously, it depends equally on not taking it personally. I can't afford to internalize it and certainly can't take it home to my family. Finding appropriate outlets for anger and frustration and doing things that make me feel joyous are vital to my ability to navigate the thorny paths of black/brown manhood.

I hope, ultimately, that I'll live as long as Mac with my mind and spirit intact. If I am blessed to do so, maybe someday I, too, will have wisdom to pass on to my younger brothers coming up behind me.

A STRANGER HANDED ME A BUSINESS CARD

Gavin Wyer

A stranger walked up and handed me a business card on which he'd written his home phone number. He introduced himself with a name I didn't recognize and welcomed me to call him anytime I needed a friend. Then he said one sentence I remember most clearly: "I could hear the pain in what you were saying." He left the room with the parting words—"Call me when you get home"—and a smile. I turned the card over and read, "Aaron Devor, Sociology Professor at the University of Victoria."

———

Eighteen months earlier, I had been home sick from work and, out of boredom, turned on my TV. I paused at a program in which Oprah Winfrey was interviewing Chaz Bono, the child of musicians Sonny and Cher. He was the first trans man I had ever seen.

I grew up in the 1950s era of Christine Jorgensen, so I knew that trans women existed—that it was somehow possible to change one's physical sex from male to female. But I had never heard of a single trans man. I had simply assumed that the transition I'd fantasized about since childhood was just that: an unfulfillable dream that I had never quite outgrown.

Suddenly, I knew it was possible and in that moment I made a decision. That night I began my internet search for pointers and found a whole new world that I never knew existed: the transgender community. And with each web page I discovered and discussion group I joined, one piece of advice appeared consistently: *Before you begin transitioning, make sure you have a solid support system in place.*

It made sense to me that support was every bit as important as good medical information, so I started building my base by telling select family, friends and a few close co-workers that I intended to transition from female to male. Everyone was understanding; the most common response I heard was, "Well, that just makes sense." It turned out that the only person who was surprised by this revelation was *me*.

I read everything I could find about gender transition; I ordered a copy of any autobiography written by a trans man. I devoured Max Wolf Valerio's *The Testosterone Files*, Matt Kailey's *Just Add Hormones,* Ryan Sallans' *Second Son*, Jamison Green's *Becoming A Visible Man* and many others. Their stories guided me through the early days of transition and affirmed that there were others out there who'd also spent years struggling with gender identity. And they confirmed that what I'd always wanted was truly possible: I could be a man.

Still, I was nervous when I met with my doctor. Though he'd been my primary care physician for close to a decade, I had never really *talked* to him. I tended to only enter a hospital if I thought my life was in jeopardy, but that had to change now.

I told him that I wanted to transition and asked if he would be comfortable enough with it to oversee all the medical aspects. His answer surprised me.

"If I'm not comfortable with this then I probably wouldn't be comfortable with a lot of things. And that wouldn't do me much good as a doctor," he stated. He also assured me that my life was about to change for the better. Later, I learned that he had helped other patients transition and was known as one of the few trans-friendly doctors in the area.

Now that I had his support, as well as that of my co-workers and friends, I was ready to begin my medical transition. I started taking testosterone and saw a gynecologist and a plastic surgeon to arrange my hysterectomy and chest reconstruction immediately.

Transitioning on the job proved remarkably easy, though I'd been fearing the worst. I had been a Corrections Officer for the past thirteen years and expected that there would be some fairly negative fallout trying to transition in such a rigid environment. But as it turned out, I experienced almost universal support; the vast majority of my male co-workers seemed quite pleased with my decision. They were quick to welcome me to the "boy's club" and use my new name and pronouns. As I began to grow facial hair and my voice dropped, I was the subject of a fair amount of teasing, none of it the least bit malicious.

Despite this, one piece was still missing from my support system: other trans men. Though I had met a couple local trans guys, we had little in common; they were in their late teens and early twenties, while I was over fifty. So, for the most part, I lived my early days of transition in isolation from older, more experienced trans men who could guide me.

———

Reading transgender discussion groups online, I had seen several conferences mentioned. I was intrigued, but they were all very far from my Canadian home and seemed to focus primarily on the needs of trans women. Then, one group started talking about Gender Odyssey, a yearly conference just close enough that I could go. It seemed to have a lot to offer men, so I made a plan with another trans man I'd met online to attend. "It'll be fun," I thought, "to be in a space with so many other guys that I could actually relate to."

I met up with John en route to Seattle and we headed off together on our adventure. He was much newer to medical transition than I, having only recently started testosterone therapy and not undergone any surgeries. I, on the other hand, had already had been on testosterone for over a year and undergone both top surgery and a hysterectomy. As I had decided against any kind of bottom surgery, meeting John reaffirmed my naive belief that I was pretty much "fully" transitioned.

I thoroughly enjoyed the first two days of Gender Odyssey. I got to meet dozens of trans men of all ages: some who, like John, were very new to transition and others who had begun decades earlier. I was surprised to meet several who identified as gay; I had only recently realized that that's how I identified, but had thought there were few others like me. I met people who identified as gender-fluid or genderqueer, which were new concepts to me. I even went to workshops on genital surgery and learned about possibilities that I had never considered.

Finally, I was somewhere I felt I belonged, where there were others like me, where I was welcomed. I was no longer alone. But while it felt wonderful to be in a place where I felt so included, I was beginning to understand just how isolated I had been—and that, after the conference, I would be returning to it. I started recognizing that I had a long way to go before I could consider myself "fully" transitioned and that to get there I needed to find a mentor.

At one workshop, I decided to talk about how it felt to be around so many trans men and how I faced the reality of returning to a small city in the Canadian Prairies where such a community did not exist and was not likely to for some time. At the end a man approached and handed me his business card. At first I was simply puzzled at why, of all the trans men there, he had chosen *me*. I wondered who he was. I wasn't even sure that he was transgender—though as I'd learned there, it was much harder to guess than expected.

When I asked John if he knew who this guy was, it turned out they came from the same city. He was actually very aware of who Aaron Devor was and had been hoping for a chance to introduce us. So, later that evening he and I walked up to Aaron at the conference picnic.

There was something about this man that drew me. He exuded a quiet confidence and had a gentle caring way about him. Over the past few days I had figured out that I needed a mentor and Aaron certainly seemed qualified. So I asked if he would be willing to mentor me. He agreed readily.

———————

After the picnic, I went back to my hotel room thinking that I would probably not call him. During our conversation, he had made several comments that gave me the impression he "read" me a whole lot more than I was comfortable with. I had a feeling I would be far more vulnerable with this man than I was willing to be with anyone else. He seemed too insightful and it terrified me. When he left early the next morning, I let out a sigh of relief. Still, I kept his card.

Later that morning I found myself in the convention center's washroom crying uncontrollably without any idea why. Now I recognize that I had moved into a new phase of transition for which I was completely unprepared: psychological and emotional turmoil. As I headed home from Gender Odyssey, my heartache only increased; once I arrived it became unbearable. Though I knew I needed help to sort out what was happening to me, I didn't want to call Aaron. He frightened me too much. But inevitably I reached a point where I knew I *had to*. I gave in and called.

During our first phone conversation, he was able to help me sort out what I was experiencing. I found myself admitting that he'd breezed past all my defenses and left me emotionally naked. In turn, he said something that shook me to the core.

"I *see* you—and you need people in your life who can truly see you."

I knew in that moment I could no longer live in seclusion. Something had to change. I'd become aware too that I was not yet a man, but an adolescent just beginning to go through the struggles that anyone must to attain true adulthood. So, over the next few weeks I made several life-altering decisions: I would leave my career and home and move across the country to where I could find a trans community.

Though Aaron tried to warn me how difficult this would be, I really didn't hear him. It was when I gave two weeks' notice at work that I began to understand. So much of my identity was wrapped up in my job; I had no idea who I would be without my uniform. As a friend and co-worker once said, "We don't choose the job. The job chooses us and we become who the job needs us to be."

With the choice to take very early retirement from Corrections also came the opportunity to withdraw what had accrued in my pension fund. Now that I had enough money to afford the bottom surgery I'd come to realize I needed, I decided to undergo a metoidioplasty. I contacted several surgeons, researched various options and settled on going to Serbia for the procedure.

———

Around this time, Aaron mentioned he was Jewish. Instantly, I thought to myself, "Oh no, please don't be Jewish, be anything but Jewish!"

Judaism had been something I'd struggled with for most of my life. Much like Aaron, it drew me in but unnerved me as well. When I was a child my mother, filled with a constant sense of seeking, had joined several religions briefly; the only one she forbade was Judaism. But as much as the other beliefs she tried on never quite fit for her, they never quite fit for me either.

The one time I did begin to explore Judaism, she had a violent reaction, deeply ingraining me with the sense that this was something I must never do again. Even as an adult I retained that fear response, yet the feeling that I was somehow connected to Judaism remained. Now suddenly that struggle was revived and I knew it was time to seek my truth.

I began to research Judaism and found that it still resonated with me as strongly as it had when I was a child. I ended up going to talk with a Rabbi who immediately understood why I felt compelled to be there and began to teach me the basic tenets of the faith. When I told Aaron about it, he said something that would never have occurred to me.

"Given your lifelong struggle with Judaism and your mother's over-the-top reaction to all things Jewish, it's very likely that you *are* Jewish."

He explained that many Jews had hidden or turned away from their ancestry as a reaction to the Holocaust, either attempting to stay safe or out of survivor's guilt. The next time I spoke to the Rabbi, he agreed that this was likely true in my case; further research proved it. Suddenly I was facing yet another identity challenge. In a matter of months I had gone from identifying as a lesbian corrections officer who practiced Paganism to an unemployed gay Jewish man who, moreover, was preparing to move across the country and then travel overseas for genital reconstruction. I was an emotional wreck.

In the shadow of all of this chaos I began packing to move. Aaron was a constant source of support throughout, telling me that if I wasn't emotionally all over the map he would be much more concerned. I sent him several emails a day during this period—I'm sure I tried his patience. The first might tell him I was a complete mess and bordering on suicidal; then, a few hours later, another message would announce how well I was doing. In between we had regular phone calls that included a great deal of crying. He listened endlessly and continued to tell me that he believed I would get through this.

———

I had been estranged from all members of my birth family for over twenty-five years with one exception: my younger sister Sandra. She had contacted me right about the time I had made the decision to transition and was immediately supportive. She was not at all surprised and even reminded me of a conversation we had had years ago in which I had mentioned feeling like a man trapped in the wrong body. I had forgotten that I ever voiced those feelings but it made sense that if I had, it would have been to her.

Now that she was back in my life, we talked on the phone daily. When I told her about my plan to get surgery, she offered me her home and her care, both before and afterwards for as long as I needed. I accepted gratefully. Her husband Mark even offered to accompany me to Serbia as a caregiver if I did not have someone else. I declined because I already had a close friend coming, but I was still humbled by his willingness.

At the end of October, I arrived on my sister's doorstep carrying all of my belongings and in a state of emotional instability. I had just one month to prepare for surgery and no idea where I would end up living or what I would be doing to earn a paycheck afterward. My only rational option was to carry on with the plan I had made when my thinking was clearer.

In early December I flew to Serbia with Jarrod, a dear trans male friend, by my side. A month earlier he had surprised me by offering to be my caregiver; it was a tremendous gift for him to travel overseas and leave his spouse for a month.

Surgery turned out to be a nightmare. Though I got exactly what I asked for—a metoidioplasty with urethral extension and testicular implants—I was completely unprepared for the grueling recovery. I had no idea that recovery would take three times longer than I expected or that those first few weeks would be more painful than anything I'd ever experienced. I developed a complication: some stitches dissolved too early and others not at all. I also experienced intense sensitivity that precluded wearing clothing below the waist.

I spent most of my time in Serbia sitting on the couch half naked and sobbing. Jarrod became my hands-on nurse; though it was much more intimate than either of us expected, he bore it stoically. When I returned to Canada, my sister took over my care. We had to take multiple trips to the local emergency room during which she directed doctors where to remove stitches and where to place new ones.

"I think this surgery might have been the biggest mistake of my life," I stated at several points. Fortunately, though, my body ultimately healed and I am quite pleased with my results today. After two months of recovery I was ready to figure out where to live and work.

I was offered a well-paying job near my sister's home but the more I thought about staying, the more depressed I felt. I realized that if I were to remain with nothing more than financial stability, I might as well have stayed in the middle of the prairies. So I took a final leap of faith and moved to Victoria, where Aaron and other trans friends lived. Though it took several months to find a job that was a good fit, I have no regrets.

Returning to Gender Odyssey after having been through my own odyssey was a kind of pilgrimage. This year there was an "Elder Track" that reminded me of two very important things: first, that my experience as a fifty-something trans man is not unique, and second, that while I've been lucky to complete a physical transition within two years, I'm still a baby within the larger process of becoming the man I want to be.

Without question this has been the most difficult year of my life; much of it felt like a free-fall with no idea where I would land. Recently,

I experienced losing contact with two of my children and three of my grandchildren. But it has also been a year of phenomenal growth, and for that I am grateful.

I have found a home in each of the communities to which I need to belong. My sister and I have reaffirmed the unbreakable bond we've shared since childhood. And as for Aaron and I: we've developed a wonderful friendship. These days, we go bike riding, we make each other laugh often and I enjoy time spent with his wife and grandson, too. I value his friendship above all others and have come to truly love the stranger who handed me a business card.

THE GLOW

Mitch Kellaway

I stir when the hotel door swings open. The sound of tiny feet padding past my bed tells me that the kids have returned with their mother. *How did these two little ones manage to awaken, dress and leave the room without me noticing?* Their entrances and exits are usually boisterous, something that I've been delighting in as a weekend visitor to this family, but which eventually draws a strained look from their parents.

I can feign sleep no longer. I place my glasses on my face just in time to witness my friend Ezra's four-year-old son Isaac launch himself onto his father's bed. His seven-year-old sister Liza quickly follows suit. They are fairly bursting with what had enabled their stealthy morning feat: "Happy Father's Day!" Their shouts draw Ezra's head out from under a pile of blankets and wriggling children. He flashes me a sleepy grin.

As the kids eagerly explain their scone selections to their father, Ezra's wife Aviva puts down a tray with three large coffees and turns to me.

"You get honorary Father's Day coffee, too," she intones, mock-ceremoniously offering me a cup. I accept this small gift gratefully, touched. I feel as if the drink has faintly anointed me with the glow of fatherhood.

Ezra's first Father's Day begins in a Philadelphia hotel room, a block away from the Transgender Health Conference that has drawn thousands to the city. While my friend has always been a man—both before *and* after his heart, body and social interactions acknowledged his deep-held truth—there is nothing quite like hearing this reflected back from the mouths of his beloved family. From where I'm perched on my adjoining hotel bed, these three words carry a special ring.

I half-listen to Isaac and Liza play a made-up game, their excited chatter escalating with holiday energy. Momentarily my thoughts drift, settling upon my brethren scattered throughout local hotels and friends' guest rooms. I marvel at the thought that there are numerous other trans men within this very town, maybe at this very moment, celebrating such an occasion—just one pinnacle amongst the many precious firsts experienced in lives where gendered liberties are not easily taken for granted.

My introspective bubble pops as the children pull me back to the moment. Unprompted, Isaac places a party hat onto his head and sings "Happy Birthday," the realization dawning a minute too late that he meant to say "father." The good intention stands as Ezra quietly excuses himself to the bathroom to dress. The kids dissolve into a make-believe session while Aviva and I watch over them, contentedly sipping.

Shortly, we are walking the streets of Philadelphia, looking for an easy, family-friendly brunch. I take the time to observe Ezra and Aviva interacting with their kids, attempting to glean hints on how to raise my own future children to be equal parts inquisitive, open-minded and respectful of reasoned limits. Meanwhile, bouncy Isaac trots ahead on an imaginative lark and Ezra gamely follows with long strides.

As his father draws near, Isaac automatically reaches up to grasp his waiting hand. My mind's eye offers a quick snapshot of myself ten years in the future, Ezra's equal in age and demeanor, possessing a presence that welcomes a small child to feel so unquestioningly protected. Father and son lead us to our planned destination, only to find that it does not keep as early hours as school-aged children do. Aviva and Ezra, ready for that moment-by-moment decision-making familiar to caretakers everywhere, forge ahead to the back-up locale.

I use the extra walk to internally dig for the best Father's Day gift I can offer: a reflection on my own upbringing. Liza, ever observant of the adults around her, spots an impending conversation. She falls in beside me to listen.

I tell Ezra that although I understand his occasional consternation at the children's unflagging curiosity—an unpredictable trait that sometimes leads them to cross personal space, both physical and mental—his parenting offers something irreplaceable. I speak from the perspective of a man whose childhood was restrained by poverty and framed by a single mother's disability and fatigue.

Ezra and Aviva's able-bodied and carefully thought-out approach allows their children freedom to explore until they reach the boundaries of their youthful comprehension. They are never shamed to ask questions emerging from received biases about gender, (dis)ability, race and employment; their parents aim only to intervene when their language is unthinkingly disrespectful or breaches privacy. Otherwise, Isaac and Liza are able to discuss observations of sexism, racism, ableism or classism others would consider "impolite" for company, rendered in their own simple language. When they reflect back their developing worldviews, these young people spill over with compassion.

Before my effusiveness threatens to embarrass him, Ezra spots the restaurant and our group settles in to eat a simple breakfast in his honor. I spend this borrowed first Father's Day brunch deep in conversation with his daughter, whose ears had immediately perked up at the mention of turbulent childhood experiences so unlike her own.

As we trade stories, I can see her struggling to paint an internal picture of me at her age; mentally walking in my shoes provides her another building block of empathy. Brow furrowed, she fires a string of queries to help her understand the man before her: born with (to use her phrase) "a body like mine," moving from apartment to shelter to apartment, holding in playful shouts to help my sick mother rest.

"Your mom must have been sad when she got sick; seeing you now must make her happy," she concludes after nearly an hour. I silently send up a wish that this child will never learn how many parents thoughtlessly lose out on the joy of knowing their own transgender sons and daughters.

She is so intent on hearing my words that her parents offer to slip out, entrusting me to keep her heart, mind and body safe. After another hour spent verbally careening between my childhood reminiscences, the dangers of cigarettes, the many kinds of artist one can grow to become and the different roles of presidents and senators, I regretfully realize that it's nearly time for me to catch my bus home from Philadelphia.

Stepping out onto the sidewalk, she grabs my hand as I steer us back to her parents. Locking eyes with a stranger as I pass, he mumbles to me, "Happy Father's Day, man." I consider stopping to explain that I am merely a temporary guardian, but instead I nod in thanks and continue onward.

FEARFULLY AND WONDERFULLY MADE

H. Adam Ackley

I am a person who has struggled with God almost my whole life, a person who has struggled primarily against myself—a confused person who frequently loses track of myself and reaches out to my Maker in desperation, trying to find and be found. Much of that confusion has been very basic, starting with my earliest memories. Back then I could not articulate why I was distraught about something that seemed so simple to everyone around me: being gendered.

Since early childhood, I had daydreamed of transitioning medically, like the trans* tennis star Renee Richards, as soon as I reached adulthood. After that I would live openly as the gay man I felt myself to be. But once I finally reached the cusp of eighteen years old, I found myself living as openly androgynous. I socialized in the gay community but was also affiliated formally with a specific religious tradition for lifelong practice; even then I desired spiritual fellowship and training.

At this tender moment, I encountered the first trans* person I'd ever met, a person entirely crushed in spirit by transphobia in the gay community and an abusive male lover. Transitioning from male-to-female proved so painful that, in despair, they had transitioned back to male again. They were deeply depressed by the whole experience and by their current life of forced gender conformity.

Nearly thirty years later, this was still the only model I had for living a transgender existence and I didn't know of any gender-variant role models in my faith community—other than, that is, a few ancient saints ridiculed or long forgotten. And I could not imagine how I, as a Protestant Christian minister and professor of Christian history and doctrine at a Christian university, could live as myself. But I also knew I could no longer stay alive otherwise, enduring the slow death of living closeted.

My whole life had become a struggle to embrace feminism and womanhood as fully as I could, frantically seeking God's help and strength to adhere to what felt so wretchedly miserable and ill-fitting that I was frequently suicidal and usually intoxicated or medicated. The more I fought against myself, the angrier I was with the unjust, uncaring God who made me a creature that could never embody my expected gender or sexuality, thus condemning me to internal torment and self-hatred.

Struggling alone with God and scriptures had not yet been enough to help me live my life fully. As I was about to turn forty-seven, my health was in a seemingly unstoppable downward spiral and the doctors I turned to persisted in administering female hormones and psychiatric medications while turning aside my requests to discuss my confusion about gender and sexuality.

Then, my last-ditch effort to find new providers and stop self-medicating yielded a different result. For the first time, my psychiatrist, psychologist, family practitioner and mentor in my spiritual recovery program for addiction all recognized that I was simply transgender. Their approach coincided with that year's changes in psychiatric standards of diagnosis and treatment, as well as strides toward legal protections for discrimination against transgender people.[1] I was finally given permission to stop identifying as a mentally ill woman and stop pursuing treatments that didn't work for a condition I didn't have.

Accepting myself as a transgender man allowed me to stay clean from all self-medicating and self-harm behaviors without the aid of psychiatric medications for the first time in decades. I regained full physical health with the strength to be a hands-on parent to my children again and even added mentoring to my teaching of students.

Having reached the brink of death due to a lifetime of addiction, self-starvation and even more aggressive violence against myself, I was now able to surrender. I stopped fighting God and considered a suggestion from the two women guides in my life: The Creator had purposely and lovingly made me trans*, not as a punishment but as a gift. My reflex, as a lifelong spiritual seeker, was to remember an ancient Hebrew scripture, a prayer of praise to God for being "fearfully and wonderfully made" with intention, just as I am (Palm 139).[2]

Even so, I had no idea how to live as a transgender person of faith, particularly in my generally homophobic and implicitly transphobic faith community. Even my recovery mentor encouraged me to continue living as a woman, afraid that the social pressures of transphobia would drive me back to active addiction. But she did refer me to a genderqueer community organizer in recovery so that I, a drowning man with no other way to cling to life, could find other trans* men. I thank God today that my cries for help were answered immediately.

I cold-called gay men and queer women in spiritual recovery and they spread the message through their social networks. Trans* men reached back to me as brothers, one after another—friends of friends of friends of people with whom I was barely acquainted. My first call cascaded into more and more calls, emails and social media "friending" of people I'd never met; each new contact, in turn, introduced me to other trans* brothers. They formed the ever-extending branches of my new trans* family tree.

As part of my own peace-centered spirituality and on the advice of allies, I sought to come out gradually—to make steady progress toward thorough and rigorous honesty without unduly triggering others, particularly those in the Christian community. To that end, before I had even started medical treatment or filed legal documents for gender and name change, I gave advance notice of several months to key people, only to receive a very transphobic backlash that resulted in a public controversy, outing me on a scale for which I was not yet ready.

My trans* brothers and sisters consistently encouraged me not to give up when it seemed my only options were to live again as a woman— which I couldn't do sober—or suicide. With support from them, as well as cisgender allies, I began to exist ever more as myself, living by faith, trusting in what I hope for and believing in what I do not yet see.[3]

Following a careful attempt to explain my impending legal name change to my employer of fifteen years—which resulted in a decision that public awareness of my transgender and gay identities had become too distracting for my work there to continue—supporters from all over the world reached out to me. Trans* brothers who share my vocation gave me hope that the loss of one job did not mean the end of my life of spiritual service and teaching.

———

When I am lost and cannot see a way forward, my impulse is to ponder Jewish and Christian stories and prayers, which serve as a road map and compass to finding my way back to myself and how I hope to live with others. For me, the model of brotherhood as I've experienced it with other trans* men is the relationship between Moses and Aaron, who led the Jewish people out of oppression and violence into a Promised Land where they could flourish. Like Moses, who struggles with self-doubt as a self-described "man of uncircumcised lips," I denied whom God has called me to be—a gay trans* man—out of fear of others' reactions, knowing I wasn't strong enough on my own to face other people's disbelief and criticism.[4]

In my case, I spent about thirty years trying to avoid this reality, throwing myself with increasing energy into being a good Christian wife and mother as I thought others of my religious community expected. During the final two years of living in gender conformity, my physical and psychological torment was so extreme that I experienced organ failure, wasting disease and was nearly dead from chronic illness. And, just as God did for Moses after temporarily afflicting him with leprosy, God demonstrated life-giving power over my fear by miraculously restoring me to full health and vigor once I accepted my transgender identity.

Moses was afraid to do what God called him to do and be who God called him to be within his own religious community. When he begged for help, God promised him the help of his older brother Aaron, who came running to embrace and support him.

God reassures Moses that Aaron will speak *for* him to other people—those who Moses rightly anticipates won't believe him—just as Moses, in turn, will speak God's words in private to his brother, whom he *does* trust. Moses pours out his heart to Aaron, sharing all God has promised, and Aaron believes him, trusting and helping his brother without hesitation or doubt. Over and over, they find their voice and strength together. At one point, Moses so exhausts himself praying that Aaron even steadies him physically all day until he can rest at sundown.

This is the kind of hands-on support my trans* brothers have consistently given me. At the lowest points of conflict with those who disagree with my affirming and inclusive interpretation of our shared religious tradition, I skipped meals and went almost three weeks without a full night's sleep. I frantically tried to calm explosive dialogues with words of peace to build unity and understanding.

Meanwhile, notes, phone calls, journal articles, prayers and blog posts from my trans* brothers, sisters and allies poured love, support and strength to me and my children when I was beyond the point of physical exhaustion. This allowed me to take one more step each day toward living with spiritual integrity, rather than crumbling or snapping.

Two trans* brothers in my spiritual recovery network even made a three-hour drive to spend time with my children and help me clean out my office when I left my job. They were like the two arms of Aaron propping me up as I faltered in fear of the future and was too overwhelmed to care alone for my children. In a note of encouragement, my newfound trans* brother Cameron, also a minister and theologian, reached out to introduce himself with these handwritten biblical verses: "See what love the Father has given us, that we should be called children of God and that is what we are. The reason the world does not know us is that it did not know Him. Beloved, we are God's children now; what we will be has not yet been revealed. What we do know is this: When He is revealed, we will be like Him, for we will see Him as He is."[5]

In my trans* brothers I see what Cameron alludes to here: hope, courage, grace and community. In them I see what I may become, how I may live, what I too may have to share and give. My trans* brothers teach me to be myself and to be a brother too—no longer with fear or shame, but with gratitude.

After forty years of wandering in the wilderness of the Sinai desert, Moses has so well learned the habit of asking brothers for help that he sends explorers ahead to assist his people in learning how to reach the Promised Land—which they do. In the same way, trans* brothers and sisters have gone before me in every kind of journey, showing me their own experiences, strength and hope. They bear witness to me that although we each transition in our own unique ways—the transgender ways God has made, the other transitions planned for us and that which one day will be fulfilled in us—our unique gendering is not to be feared but rather to be celebrated as good and nourishing.

Just as Moses encouraged the people of Israel, so my trans* brothers remind me not to be afraid and to remember that God has gone before us, fought for and borne us, because God is the One Who loves and chooses us just as we are. And so our Creator, Deliverer and Redeemer brings us out of the bondage of transphobia and through the wilderness—of gender dysphoria and whatever other forms of transition we may experience—to fulfill the promise of what we shall become.

HIDING BEHIND HUMOR

Dustin Ashizz

Miguel has very few teeth remaining, having grown up poor in Mexico City only one block from the shanty town huts where people even poorer struggle to survive another day. He is now a self-taught chef for a small deli and catering business in the greater metropolitan New York area. Justly proud of his hard won achievements, he has no idea that he has also shepherded me into the world of jocular male bonding.

I am the short, deaf, overeducated American-Israeli Jewish guy from a privileged background who washes dishes in the kitchen of that deli and catering business. At my next birthday, I will be sixty-years-old. And although I have identified as male since I can remember, appropriate medical treatment was denied me until I was age fifty-four.

My body has responded with vigor to receiving the testosterone it needed for so long, but it is impossible to ever catch up to the physical condition I would have been in had I received treatment earlier in life. My beard is that of a typical twenty-year-old man. I look like a kid. My skeleton betrays the influence of female hormones, giving me a perpetually baby-faced appearance on top of shoulders that are too narrow. I must be sure that some of my thinning gray hair sticks out from under my head covering or else my age will be challenged in liquor stores.

Since having only recently experienced all the effects of a second puberty, even I have trouble thinking of myself as a grown-up. Miguel refuses to believe that I am two decades older than his forty years. He calls me *niño* ("baby boy") and teases me good-naturedly about my boyishly thin, weak arms and jokingly recommends that masturbating more often will strengthen them. I tease him back, saying, "That's not true, Miguel. If it were true, my arms would be ten times bigger and stronger than yours!"

Despite my deafness, I have no problem communicating with Miguel. He is a master of visual-spatial-tactile dimensions and speaks through his hands with exceptional competence. The third member of our kitchen brotherhood—Diego, a thirty-four-year-old sous chef—also hails from Mexico City and is naturally talented at mime.

Between the three of us, we have developed our own hybrid language composed of elements taken from Spanish, English, American Sign Language, Mexican gesture and mime. It is primarily a silent, visual system of hand gestures, but it includes some spoken words. I call it "Spanglish Mime Sign."

Since I didn't become deaf until I was around twenty-seven-years-old, I retain fairly good speech skills and I use them in trying to speak some Spanish. Miguel and Diego's native tongue happens to be one of the easiest in the world to lip-read, so it is helpful to encourage them to speak Spanish to me. I could never understand what Miguel was saying when he asked me to fetch celery, but as soon as he taught me the Spanish word *apio*, we were in business.

To satisfy Miguel's expansive and insistent curiosity about everything, I've also taught him some Hebrew, but my language is notoriously difficult to lip-read and he is disappointed when I cannot understand his words even though he says them correctly. We mostly stick to our Spanglish Mime Sign. And we mostly talk about sex.

I suspect that this perpetual focus on sex got started because Miguel and Diego were so amused by my reactions to their lewd jokes. As a recently transitioned trans man, I had never been around guys who were joking about masturbating and having intercourse and I had no idea how I was expected to respond. All I could do was laugh. Miguel and Diego began to compete with each other to elicit the greatest shocked and embarrassed laughter from the strange little Jew who was unlike any other guy they had ever met.

For months, I did not trust myself to offer a retaliatory joke. I enjoyed the camaraderie, but I was scared of doing or saying the wrong thing and accidentally revealing that I was a middle-aged novice to the Brotherhood of Crude Sexual Joking. *How could I speak and joke confidently about a physical embodiment I have never experienced? What if I made a sexual gesture that wasn't quite the way a cisgender man would make it? How was I to decode the sociocultural protocol governing the erotic jokes Miguel and Diego had grown up knowing but which I had never encountered?*

Like a bunch of adolescents, we have found ample fodder for sexualized humor in vegetables. I inadvertently launched the tradition of playing with produce one day when I noticed a remarkably large, phallic-looking carrot on Miguel's cutting block. I simply picked it up and stared at it for a moment, then turned my gaze to meet Miguel's and quietly murmured, *"¡Ai yi yi!"* He exploded in a torrent of laughter and Spanish spoken directly to Diego, who also bent over in amusement.

Later, I learned that they had set the carrot out as bait to see if I would react to its size and shape and, much to their delight, I had fallen for it. Thereafter, Miguel took to sneaking up and surprising me as I washed dishes, suddenly revealing some sort of vegetable hidden under his apron. Eggplants, parsnips, celery and even string beans all fell prey to his humor.

For months I rewarded them with appreciative chuckles while remaining a passive participant, for I still had no self-confidence in making my own sex jokes. A turnaround came one day when Miguel greeted me with another large carrot, held at his crotch and flanked by two small cherry tomatoes. Snickering in satisfaction at my responsive groan, he danced in victory back to his preparation table where Diego was busy peeling potatoes. Realizing this was my opportunity, I marched over, took the hapless carrot from Miguel and replaced the diminutive cherry tomatoes with two huge potatoes.

"¡He aquí!" ("Behold!"), I proclaimed.

Judging from the duration and intensity of their laughter, I knew I had done the right thing. Since then, I have participated much more actively in the ancient male bonding tradition of having phallic fun with food. It was a great day for me when, with a perfectly straight face and steady gaze, I became sufficiently emboldened to loudly crush an empty egg shell held at my groin, thereby meeting the implied challenge Miguel had been giving me for months as he pranced around taunting me with waist-level eggs.

———

After almost a year of this banter, I am still blindsided by their cisgenderisms more often than I like to admit. In the wintery days following a blizzard, Miguel coined a new Spanglish Mime Sign as he described the numbing cold he felt while digging his car out from three feet of snow. As he curled his index finger inward and grimaced, I instantly understood his new sign to mean "penis-shriveling cold."

I have long known that cisgender men's genitalia retracts when exposed to extreme cold, but this is not something I have experienced directly. I'll never know the sensation because all I have is a prosthesis that cannot feel temperature. I can use it to "write my name in the snow," as the saying goes, but it cannot perceive the cold.

It would never have occurred to me to describe my experience as "penis-shriveling." So although I understood the meaning of Miguel's sign, all I could do was smile and nod. Diego, on the other hand, immediately loved the gesture and it has quickly become the new standard to describe feeling frigid. The two of them began to routinely use it as a commentary on their time spent working inside the kitchen's coolers and freezers.

For my part, I tried to avoid this particular line of banter because I simply could not know how to accurately portray a believable experience. To my dismay, Miguel eventually challenged me. Upon returning to the kitchen from taking the garbage out to the dumpster, he made a show of describing exactly how penis-shriveling cold it was outside. Since I'd often poked fun at him for being hypersensitive to the cold, he jokingly demanded that I take out the next load of garbage and see how *my* penis could withstand the temperature.

Not quite thinking things through, I turned and began to wheel out the next garbage can, neglecting to put on my coat. In my thin T-shirt and sneakers, I morosely pushed the bin through the snow, wondering what I was going to say to Miguel and Diego when I returned.

Trudging back towards the kitchen, I realized that my only recourse was to make an outrageously ridiculous joke at my own expense. Hoping that my powerfully built, brown-skinned colleagues would not see that my thin, pale arms had turned blue, I swaggered back into the kitchen. Devilishly grinning with expectation, the two closely watched my return.

"So, how's your dick?" Miguel asked me in Spanglish Mime Sign. Knocking aside the empty garbage can, I struck a dramatic pose and said out loud in my limited Spanish, *"¡Mi salchichon es caliente!"* ("My sausage is hot!") Continuing, I signed, "It is so hot, I had to stick it in the snow to cool it down!"

Thankfully, my attempt at male humor was well received and the two of them dissolved into laughter; I think I even saw them nod their heads in approval. This is typical of my joking strategy with Miguel and Diego—one akin to that of a thirteen-year-old boy. Since I cannot ever know how to make sexual jokes that mirror actual cisgender male experience, my jokes must be preposterous by default.

Another day, as Miguel was telling me how many carrots to prepare for the coleslaw, he made a tangential jab at Diego in Spanglish Mime Sign.

"If the carrots are big like me he said," indicating his penis, "get two of them. But if they're small like Diego, get eight."

"You're out of your mind, Miguel!" Diego mimed in protest. I felt a flash of panic as they both turned to me for a response. Somehow, the answering signs formed on my hands.

"Okay, so if the carrots are like Diego, I'll get eight. If they're like you, I'll get two. And if they're like me, I'll cut one in half." Miguel doubled over in a belly laugh and Diego gave me a mimed rim shot in reward.

———————

I am both pleased and relieved when Miguel and Diego appreciate my humor, but I am constantly aware that these are the kind of jests I would have been making decades ago had the conditions of my birth been different. My jokes are funny because they present such absurd contradictions to the obvious reality. I am small, weak and effeminate. Although my voice can reach into the baritone range, my speech habits and body language stubbornly reflect my early female socialization, much to my chagrin.

I suspect that Miguel and Diego wondered if I was gay when I first arrived. They asked me a lot of questions about my relationships with women, to which I made a point of letting them know that I had had a wife for decades. Though true, it's likely not quite in the way they think. They don't realize that the woman to whom I was married was strictly a lesbian. She ended our thirty-year relationship when I began to transition, preferring the companionship of a "real woman."

I've also deliberately misled Miguel and Diego into thinking that I watch heterosexual pornography on my computer. In actuality, the conditioning of my orthodox Jewish background makes me shy away from it. Still, something in me wants these two men to think that I indulge in watching so I don't deny it when they ask if I do. Perhaps I imagine they will think I am more of a "normal" man than I will ever be if they believe that I enjoy porn.

Every day, I spend hours washing pots that are bigger than I am. My duties include moving sacks of potatoes and boxes of meat weighing more than half of my total body weight. Miguel and Diego do these things easily while I struggle to find optimal leverage points, usually having to kneel on the floor in order to raise my burden.

Because they are kind and gentle men, they do not make fun of me in a cruel way when they see me struggle. They watch from the corners of their eyes only to gauge if I need help, allowing me space to do things by and for myself. I like to imagine that they even feel a bit of admiration that I can find ways to do physical tasks that are so difficult for me.

At home after work, I am exhausted. I don't even think much anymore about the advanced graduate degrees I hold and how it happens that I'm reduced to washing dishes at this stage of my life. In rare serious moments, I share some of these feelings with Miguel and he has shared some of his inner feelings with me. Ever observant, he notices when I am in a particularly hopeless mood and he makes an extra special effort to make me laugh.

Sometimes I just glare back at him and say out loud and in sign, "*Mateme, por favor.*" ("Kill me, please.") He signs back, "No, I am your friend and Diego is your friend. We laugh a lot here at work and tonight you can look at big boobs on the computer and have a good, long wank. You see: your life is not so bad!"

This always makes me smile. But when I slip off my prosthesis and wash it before going to bed, I am not smiling. I immerse it in steaming hot soap and water to clean it from the day's accumulation of urine and sweat and I think, "Yes, this is, indeed, a 'hot sausage.'" Remembering the silly jokes I've made at work portraying a body and sexuality my brain expects to be there but which never actually materializes, I confront the biggest joke of all: the naked truth.

WITHOUT LOU, WHO WOULD I BE?

Brice D. Smith

I first met Lou Sullivan (1951-1991) in the library of the University of Wisconsin-Milwaukee. I was looking for a research topic for a graduate course on gender in United States history—the first such course I had taken. The year was 2004.

Books on transgender anything took up approximately three feet on one shelf in the library and it seemed that one-third of them referenced Lou. Folks like Jamison Green, Patrick Califia, Kate Bornstein, Jason Cromwell and Leslie Feinberg all wrote of the significance of this gay trans man from Milwaukee who died in San Francisco in 1991 from AIDS complications. The little I was able to find on him had a profound and visceral effect on me.

Once I read the definitive work on Lou—Susan Stryker's article, "Portrait of a Transfag Drag Hag as a Young Man: The Activist Career of Louis G. Sullivan," I found myself still thirsting for more.[1] Who *was* this guy? How did he come to be? And how could an autographed copy of the book he had written, *From Female to Male: The Life of Jack Bee Garland*, be shelved in the general collection and forgotten, rather than encased in Special Collections?[2]

I emailed Susan Stryker and expressed my desire to learn more about Lou. She encouraged me to write his biography as she had moved on to other projects.[3] It was late spring and I applied to UWM's new

History PhD program, now determined to learn how to write a biography worthy of this remarkable man.

Lou came into my life at a pivotal time, as he had with hundreds, if not thousands, of my trans brothers in the 1980s. I had recently begun identifying as trans and considering the possibility of transitioning. The idea of transitioning excited me and being trans provided a framework for better understanding many of my thoughts, feelings and experiences.

Lou provided me with much needed validation. And courage, for I was apprehensive about challenges that transitioning might engender and fearful that no one would love me. But if this man could live as a gay FTM when such a thing supposedly did not exist and go to such extraordinary lengths to be who he was, why couldn't I?

The turning point for me came one summer night in 2008 while transcribing Lou's diaries. Lou was recounting a letter he had written to his former lover in 1979 regarding his desire to begin transitioning. He wrote:

> Now that I'm alone, I see that, if it *is* true that we are all responsible for our own happiness, that we cannot expect others to fulfill us and in the end we only have ourselves, then I better make peace with the feelings inside me. If I don't it will be the only thing on my deathbed I will regret not doing.[4]

I experienced a wave of goose bumps, moved back from my computer and asked myself, "If I were on my death bed, would I regret not transitioning?" A sea of calm passed over me as I answered, "Yes." In that moment I began embracing my identity as a trans man instead of resisting it.

———

By the time I decided to begin transitioning in 2008, I'd already spent several years intermittently attending FORGE's peer support group meetings for those along the FTM spectrum and significant others, friends, family and allies.[5] The importance of seeing other trans people and being with those who understood me cannot be overstated. The explosion of online videos by trans people about trans people attests to the desire for seeing and being seen. Like support groups, these videos can alleviate one's sense of isolation, though their primary purpose is experience-sharing.

I came to find, however, that attending meetings or otherwise spending time in the presence of trans people somehow prevented their experiences from being my own—I could identify with them, but they were experiences embodied by separate entities in shared physical space. On the other hand, the narratives recounted in online videos could be absorbed in private spaces—spaces where I could reflect and explore my inner self.

Similarly, to understand and embrace my own identity, I needed both the intimacy of Lou's experiences and innermost thoughts and feelings and the distance provided by their disembodiment. I needed to be able to identify with another trans man in solitude, through reading Lou's diaries and letters, before I could do so in a community. I needed to think about his narrative and respond to it with feeling; to embody it by proxy.

Though I may have experienced ambivalence regarding my own identification and trans narrative in my early years of work on Lou Sullivan, I never questioned the validity or importance of his. By virtue of writing a biography, one is declaring a subject's significance and helping others to see it. Lou's significance had been made apparent to me by his peers—my elders—who left a record of him in the early works of what is now Transgender Studies.

It seemed all of our prominent forebears either knew or knew of Lou Sullivan and had been shaped by both his life and his death. In fact, I would argue that the timing of Lou's death did not merely coincide with the birth of the transgender movement as we know it today, but helped to usher it in. His death gave the movement's movers and shakers, old and new, cause to reflect. Whether in public eulogies or private thought, they contemplated the role Lou had played in their lives and the lives of countless others, what it meant to be transgender, where the movement had come from and where it was going and the roles they wished to play moving forward.

The support I received from our community's elders in working on Lou's biography was overwhelming. They needed no convincing of the significance of this work, for they had lived it. The challenge at hand, as I saw it, was in convincing the transgender movement's latest generation of movers and shakers of not only Lou Sullivan's significance, but the importance of history.

How much quicker and better our collective advancement could be if we greased the wheel instead of spending our resources reinventing it! When we roll out the tribulations and triumphs of those who came before us, we discover a map for our uncharted experiences. Part of Lou's significance lay in the fact that he was one of the first trans people to educate medical professionals about their trans patients and the care they sought, one of the first trans men to publish works on trans men, to organize meetings of trans men and be a point of contact for people, trans and cisgender alike. In these ways every single trans man follows in Lou's footsteps at least once in his life to this day and does so in his own individual way.

As it turned out, the transgender movement's latest vanguard took little convincing. In fact, they were eager for role models and a sense of history and Lou's story seemed to have as profound and visceral effect on them as it did on me. My work on Lou served as an entry point into the company of the transgender movement's leaders in thought, action, and creative production and assured my membership in the trans brotherhood.

Lou had not only come into my life at a pivotal time, he became pivotal to my life. I was reclaiming our history, doing something important for our community. I was Lou Sullivan's biographer. Lou had become responsible for my mattering, both literally and figuratively.

———

In early 2009, Sean Dorsey invited me to attend the premier of Fresh Meat's *The Diary Project*, featuring a suite of dances titled "Lou," as his personal guest. The theater was packed, the performance beautiful and the work was very well-received. But I found the experience disturbing. It was difficult seeing another's interpretation of Lou. *That* Lou was not the one I had been thinking, writing, speaking about for years. I looked around and thought, "Nobody on stage or in the audience knows who he really was." The fact was neither did I.

Despite our greatest efforts at objectivity and remaining as true to the evidence as possible, the work of historians is inherently subjective. Lou left behind a wealth of information, which he bequeathed to the GLBT Historical Society, including thirty years of diaries, hundreds of letters, photographs and videotaped interviews. I fancied myself a puzzle master, fitting all of these pieces together and placing them into greater historical context, quoting Lou extensively, sticking to the narratives he told about his own life and removing my voice as much as possible. But ultimately I was telling a story and interpreting his life and its meaning.

After receiving his AIDS diagnosis, many pleaded with Lou to set aside his work on Jack Garland's biography and work on his own life story; in the years following his death, many more bemoaned the fact that Lou never did. But in dying and not leaving a definitive account of his life, Lou can live on in the imaginations of countless trans men. He can become a part of us all because there is not an actual physical Lou to make us aware of our separateness. By leaving behind a record of himself in pieces, he can mean something different to many different people. And our picking up these pieces makes us part of a greater whole. A brotherhood united in diversity.

It took me awhile to come to this realization and to realize that becoming an expert on Lou Sullivan was a part of my life's journey but not my reason for being. I had been living vicariously through him rather than living my own reality and intellectualizing his experiences had distanced me from the emotions I felt about *my* experiences. In telling his story I was discounting my own—the only story on which I could ever be an actual expert.

I wanted to believe there was a reason for my being trans and that that reason was to help others by way of Lou's story. Without Lou, who would I be?

If it is true that we are all responsible for our own happiness, that we cannot expect others to fulfill us, and in the end we only have ourselves, then I better make peace with the feelings inside me.

These words of Lou's took on new meaning. I needed to confront my fears of being who I was, of my life being meaningless and of becoming invisible again. It was time for another transition, time to be who I was in my own right—a concept Lou understood well.

———

After completing my dissertation in 2010, I walked away from my life's work to work on my life. While there was tremendous pressure to publish Lou's biography, I needed to create my own life experiences and engage with them fully. In liberating myself from my source of liberation, I found my own voice—the one you hear here. Lou had helped free me from the binds of society, but then I proceeded to bind myself to him and our community. I did so through narrative—*his* narrative.

As a trans person and historian I value narrative highly. In fact, narrative *is* history. But narrative is not, and can never be, the whole story. Narrative/history is dynamic, for the past exists only in terms of what we make of it in the present. The danger and fallacy of narrative lies in its eclipse of the experiential. On the surface such eclipsing makes sense, as narrative is the encapsulation of experiences. But the true power of narrative lies in how we experience it.

Historically, narrative has played a central role in the lives of trans people. While narrative inherently includes the sharing of experiences, it differs from experience-sharing *per se* in its intentionality. Narratives not only have a beginning and an end, but also serve as a means to an end. In the case of those who transition, narrative plays the necessary function of validating our trans identities, primarily for the medical and legal professions, but also for the larger public. Through narrative we attempt to explain to others why we are trans and, by extension, what it means to be trans.

In contrast, experiences are unscripted. They may contain common themes—others' disconcerting responses to our presence in restrooms, whispers and accusations of strangers who are uncertain of our gender loved ones surprising us with strong support of our transitions—but they are individually experienced and our experiences simply *are*. We may bind them into narratives, but our narratives can and should evolve over time, adapting to our lived experiences. We are not our narratives, but rather their authors.

Had Lou written a definitive narrative of his life, it would have constrained our imaginations, our desire to make meaning out of his life and our ability to experience him here and now. More importantly, it would have constrained him, bound him to the past when his future was knowingly limited. Lou was free to experience more, share those experiences and record them in his diaries right up to his death. And by doing so we have a better understanding not only of the remarkable life of Lou Sullivan, but what it means to be human. For there is nothing more human than contemplating death and what it means to truly live.

How we experience things, when and where we experience them and the unique combination of our experiences is what makes us who we are. And as I see it, the greatest gift of being trans is how acutely aware we are of our experiences. We have spent years struggling to understand, articulate and embody our senses of self and attained a high level of self-awareness in the process. It is good when/if our experiences matter to others, but what is most important is that they matter to *us*, for through these experiences we ascribe meaning to our lives.

I have returned to Lou's biography and begun preparing my dissertation for publication because the experience of writing about Lou has been, and continues to be, meaningful for me. Experiences encapsulated in his narrative validate mine. But this work—Lou's narrative—is not *me*. It is not Lou, nor is it you either.

So in the end, it is my hope that like Lou and myself, you will experience his narrative. But then I hope you put it down and enjoy the experience of being the extraordinary individual you are.

PART IV
NEW TERRITORY

NEW TERRITORY

Jack Sito

It's true that people always know your personal business when you live in a small town. I grew up in a rural part of Northern California, the son of Mexican immigrant parents. I am a Chicano man: the first generation of my family born in the United States, fluent in both English and Spanish. Throughout my childhood, my working-class mother and father toiled hard to provide for my younger brother and me. Thanks to their sacrifices I became the first of our family to graduate from college.

I have always felt and known that I was male since preschool when, at only two-years-old, I met Lety and Lulu, twin sisters who would wear the same exact outfit in red and blue: a dress with white polka dots and a ribbon in their hair. I tried to kiss them both by the slide during recess. For me, understanding my gender has partly been a matter of how it relates to others: I knew I was male because I was attracted to girls as a boy was. I knew I was male because when I played with other boys, I was one of them.

As I grew older, I always carried my purple sack of marbles so I would be ready to play "shoot-em-out of the circle" with the other guys. You could rely on finding a water gun and fake police badge in my pocket just in case I was needed in neighborhood games of "cops and robbers." I remember trying to pee while standing like my male friends. I would climb trees with them, too, though I alone was admonished by my teacher and mother for destroying my dress as it got caught in the branches.

What a struggle it was for my mother to dress me on a daily basis! Every morning I would plead and cry until I got to wear blue jeans and my Superman t-shirt with sneakers, rather than a pink dress. Eventually, my father tired of seeing me fight my mother each day and took me shopping for clothes I actually wanted to wear. Family friends and neighbors assured my parents that this was just a "tomboy" phase I would outgrow. But as I hit puberty, I could clearly see the way my body was developing did not match my true gender.

Once I was in college, I came out as a lesbian after having my first relationship with a woman. In hindsight, I don't believe that I ever really *was* a lesbian—the identity was merely a stepping stone on the way to who I truly was. Knowing I was attracted to women but being stuck in a female body led to that label. It would take me a long time to realize this.

Before I did, I spent years agonizing over coming out as gay to my family. I finally did it when I cut my hair short. As it turned out, my father had a hunch that I was coming home to tell them the weekend that I did. When I arrived, he had already warned my mother to brace for the news.

I had waited so long because I knew it would be hard for my parents to accept what people would think about me. In our community, being a *marimacha* or *machorra*—a "butch" Latina lesbian—carried a negative social stigma. My mother feared what people would say when I was seen in public holding or kissing another female. Moreover, living in a small town riddled with gangs and daily violence meant I risked being ridiculed, harassed and quite possibly assaulted for being a *marimacha*. I considered myself lucky that, at the very least, my parents supported me.

After graduating from college I traveled and studied in Europe for a year while preparing for law school. It was there, at age twenty-three, that I encountered Marci, the girl who would tell me what I always knew deep down: I was a man. I met her at the internet café I frequented to work on my applications and we started dating soon thereafter.

"Why haven't you transitioned to become a man yet?" she asked me one day.

"That's not possible," I responded, perplexed. Although I had been involved with gay youth support groups, attended pride festivals and was generally aware that transgender people existed, never in a million years had I thought *I* could be among them. But once Marci gave me a name—or better yet, an *answer*—to who I really was, I felt as if I was lifting a blindfold I'd been wearing for years.

So I spent the rest of my time in Europe living as a man without any surgeries or medical intervention. I already "passed" as male and was often called "sir" by strangers—or, even more often, "young man." In the youth hostels I began sleeping in the boy's dormitory; in public I started using men's bathrooms. When no one questioned me, I realized that I had finally figured out who I was. *Living as a man was truly possible.*

Upon returning to the United States, I started law school in California and regularly visited San Francisco's LGBT Center. Soon I found a therapist and support group for trans men; I read books and met with doctors with the hope that they could help me become the man I now knew I was.

I felt compelled to do research into my health and background, so I requested a DNA chromosome test and had several other exams to ascertain my body's testosterone levels before I altered them. I had a lot of unanswered medical questions: *Why was I already passing as male without medical intervention? Why had others always seen me as male while growing up?* I was certain something had gone wrong at birth: I had been born without the right male anatomical parts. Beginning my transition at age twenty-five was my way of correcting my body to match the one I should have been born with.

I came out to my parents for the second time in our same cramped living room. It was difficult to look at them and say that I was wrong, that *this time* I had figured out I was actually transgender; it was difficult to know that they had to go through the same emotions all over again. They cried and asked questions and I did the best I could to explain with all that I had learned. Though it took time and meeting with a therapist who explained what Gender Identity Disorder meant[1], my parents were ultimately, yet again, understanding and loving.

Once they comprehended that I was transitioning—and that, moreover it was not their fault—my parents were more accepting of me as a trans man than they were of me as a lesbian. Perhaps this was because society would now view me as just another Chicano male and not as a troublesome *marimacha*. Perhaps it was the thought that in the eyes of passersby, I would appear to be a "normal" Chicano son. Through them, I experienced the first glimpses of how society would perceive and embrace me: I would no longer be an outcast or fear physical harm for being a butch Latina lesbian. I could just blend in with the Latino males surrounding me.

———

As a woman, I was often called fat. I was Sasquatch or Bigfoot or any number of mean-spirited names used to describe my being overweight. As a man, I have a "beer belly"; people even tell me it's cute. I stand six feet tall, have broad shoulders, and most of my 270 pounds are around my midsection. I'm covered in hair from my arms to my legs to my thick, dark eyebrows—partly due to ethnicity and partly due to what my father jokingly calls "The Curse of the Werewolf." That curse led my mother and aunt to place me at age eleven in a tub with Nair covering my legs; I still remember the burning sensation as my hair was chemically singed off. I would cry when I had to get my eyebrows waxed and trimmed so they wouldn't resemble my father's unkempt ones. And the kids at school still teased me for being too hairy.

I wear a men's size twelve shoe—fourteen in women's—a larger size than even my brother or my father. Thank goodness I only ever had to wear two pairs of special-ordered size fourteen's in my life! As a man, it's a blessing to have big feet; I can tell what women are trying to gauge by looking at my shoes.

In fact, all of my former womanly "handicaps" are now advantages. Perhaps it's partly because I'm a big guy, perhaps it's partly because I'm

Chicano. But it's *definitely* because I'm a man. Male privilege is something I've come to realize I have and it's undeniably enjoyable.

As a man I've worked in every job I wanted; I no longer have to deal with the gatekeepers of the employment world. Before transitioning, I worked for a Public Defender's Office as a Spanish-English interpreter and was eager to become one of the firm's investigators. I looked forward to going on stake-outs, doing investigation work and interviewing those who'd witnessed crimes. But when I approached my boss about joining the team, he told me the work was too dangerous.

"It's better for you to stick with being an interpreter. It's safer for a woman," he explained. At the time, I accepted his pronouncement because I didn't know any better.

While attending college as a woman, I would share my opinions in class discussions and afterwards hear comments, mostly from male classmates.

"Miss Know it All."

"She's an opinionated bitch."

While attending law school as a man I would share my ideas and also get comments from male classmates.

"That guy is smart!"

"He really knows his stuff."

This experience allowed me to realize how other people's opinions are based significantly on social structures like race and socioeconomic class, but particularly on *gender*. As a man, I'm undoubtedly more respected by my peers. People really listen to what I have to offer.

Today, I can proudly say I've been an investigator for a Public Defender's Office for nine years. In addition, I hold a California Private Investigator's License. I work on serious homicides, shootings, stabbings, gang-related homicides, bank robberies, rapes, sexual assaults and many other serious felony cases.

I have since talked to that former boss who tried to convince me that interpreting was my place. He told me, of course, that he would now hire me as an investigator. I couldn't help but be surprised to hear this from him because, after all, I am the same capable person I was in the past. But a simple change in gender suddenly means I can perform the job.

After finishing law school I received my Juris-Doctorate degree and have since begun the process of becoming a licensed attorney. Even in a highly educated field like law, I still come across such disparities. It is unfortunate and sad to see unnecessary differences between men and women in employment, pay, socially acceptable manners, looks and roles. I truly dislike the fact that I gained more status, visibility, acceptability, income, job prospects and respect only after transitioning to manhood. After all, I know what it feels like to be on the other side of that coin.

Still, I know I have taken my new male privilege and used it to my advantage. It is a fine line that I now walk: I have to make sure that when I do accept all of the social advantages that come with being a large, educated, straight, Chicano man that I also do not forget what it was like to be a large, lesbian, Chicana woman. I can't say if ultimately walking that fine line will actually help blur it or help both sides better understand the realities of inequality. For now, I'm simply embracing what comes with the new territory.

CROSSING THE LINE

James C.K.

From what I remember about my childhood, I was a relatively carefree kid. Long before cell phones, household internet and cyber-bullying, I loved sports, playing video games, throwing rocks at those little green army men, getting into trouble and reading choose-your-own adventure stories. I was always getting dirty, always playing too rough. One recess in grade school, I broke a girl's arm while playing Red Rover. She eventually forgave me when I signed her bright green cast, but the other students never forgot the day running on the playground was outlawed and who had caused it.

If I think hard enough, I recall an ever-present white noise of parents and teachers telling me to be more careful or that I should "play nice." It was a static surrounding me, but the words never fully made sense. Barbies, My Little Ponies, costume jewelry and playing house—such playthings were mind-boggling. For the longest time, I thought maybe I was lacking in imagination; everyone else was having so much fun and I just couldn't find any joy playing those games. Friends' parents, teachers and every adult I knew continually explained the difference between boys and girls; I can only imagine my own parents were hoping that I would somehow realize I was confused. But I knew who I was and how I felt—I was really a boy like all of my friends—and they were the ones who were mistaken.

As frustrating as this was, I was blessed in that I could walk the line between genders from a very early age. I started "passing" as a boy before I ever set my mind to do so. I never gave myself a new name or demanded to be called by male pronouns; it happened organically. When I would say my name, people naturally heard another. I often didn't correct them, because I liked what they said better than my given name.

I was extremely fortunate my parents didn't force me to wear traditionally gender-appropriate clothing or play with only stereotypical "girl" toys. I was allowed to run around in dirty tennis shoes, torn jeans, baseball caps and sport a rattail. The latter was much to the amusement of my sisters, who would try to braid it occasionally. At eight-years-old I was living a double life.

Then puberty rolled around and I was still coming home with scraped knees and filthy jeans. So my parents made the decision they thought they had to: they enrolled me in an all-girl's school, complete with a plaid skirt uniform.

"It's for your own good," they assured me. I cried every day for about a year. Ironically, it was the most stereotypically feminine thing about me: crying.

My protests never made a difference, though—I still had to get up and put on my uniform, I still had to go to class with girls. So eventually I stopped. Still, I couldn't stand the idea of wearing a skirt. It felt wrong. When I walked through the halls or sat awkwardly at my desk, my biker shorts peeked out from under my uniform. I could feel my classmates' eyes on me and I thought they were always laughing. This continued for years.

But outside of school, when strangers would sometimes guess my birth gender, "female" was usually as their second thought. "Oh, I'm so sorry," they would say. At the time, misgendering was an embarrassment I can't even describe. It was as if I was standing naked and people were looking on and poking fun. So I tried growing my hair out and dressing femininely at night too. It didn't last long, though. And it certainly didn't ease my embarrassment—it was exasperated. I still felt naked, uncomfortable in my skin.

By my twenties, I finally admitted that I couldn't bear walking the line between maleness and femaleness any longer. I began drawing my own by living as a man almost full-time. The biggest, and by far the most confusing, change was in how others' perception of me went from "hyper-masculine boi" to "strangely feminine boy"—and how it all changed almost overnight.

Suddenly, I was weird for talking with my hands or not making direct eye contact. Babies and puppies and kittens weren't "cute," and if I said so I was gay. My handshake was weak and I was too quiet. If I asked for directions or an explanation, I was an idiot. If I needed help, I was pathetic.

Times have changed since my parents' were young, but modern society still has a long way to go. You take a woman who is strong, confident and knows what she wants, and she is trying to be a man. You take a man who shows any form of emotion besides anger, thinks twice and who doesn't know exactly what he wants, and he is a failure.

While interacting with others confused me, *I* knew I was done trying to "act" like a boy and had to now take the steps to legally and medically become one. I began taking testosterone shortly thereafter. Abruptly, my age changed, too. I was fourteen again, only this time with a cracking voice. Though in my late twenties, I was getting carded for rated-R movies. At the tailor, I was assured I should cuff my slacks so that I could grow into them. It was hard for him to believe that at 5'7", I had reached my full height and that my father wasn't paying for my suit.

Correcting people about my gender and age wasn't a new phenomenon and it quickly became unnecessary. After a few short months, I was back to passing without trying. Entire weeks went by where I forgot I was transgender. I was finally becoming comfortable in my own skin, even with the T-induced acne and patchy facial hair. And I relished the new me: obsessing over every whisker, trying out new styles of clothing and hair and even joining a gym.

Working out for those first few weeks, I used the men's locker room without incident. And then one day, with my back to the room and a towel draped strategically around my shoulders, I was—and it feels silly to be saying this—*teased*. I know this would have been nothing if I had grown up in boys' locker rooms, but I was horrified.

"He must have something to hide," an older man joked to another as he pointed at me. They laughed as I hurriedly pulled my shirt on and tried to keep myself from turning beet red. Having not undergone any sort of gender-confirmation surgery yet, I feared being attacked and bringing shame to my entire family when they printed my birth name in the newspaper after I died.

Grabbing my gym bag, I didn't even bother to zip it or put on my shoes. I walked as fast as possible to the exit, cursing the gym for not having a back door. *What did they see? Do they know? Am I going to have to fight? Could I possibly win?* Anxious thoughts reverberated in my head.

My nervousness only produced roaring laughter from my gym buddies. They apologized disingenuously between cackles and knee slaps. I breathed a tremendous sigh of relief as I closed the door behind me.

———

That was the second time I was truly scared for my life. The first was when I was twenty-two but still looked like an adolescent, several years before I started taking hormones.

I was out with friends at a local bar on a crowded Friday night. Everyone was calling me Nick, which was the name most strangers heard even though it sounded nothing like what I was saying. The place was packed, but we were all having a good time dancing and taking turns riding the massive mechanical bull stationed in the back of the room. It stopped being fun when I had to use the restroom.

I knew I couldn't use the men's because there was only a trough. So I told my friend Mary to come with me to the ladies' room. She agreed, laughing; she knew I would be an amusing contrast to the girls filling the bar, wearing their skirts and dresses or tight jeans with halter-tops.

Everything seemed calm while we were waiting in line as we talked about so-and-so's failed attempt on the bull and how we could do so much better. When a stall was free, I ran right in before anyone could say anything. But when I came out, Mary was nowhere to be seen.

All eyes were on me as a drunk fool started screaming at me for being in the wrong bathroom. Wordlessly, I started for the door and she threw her drink at me. As she got in my face, waving her finger and carrying on, I tried to sidestep around her. Meanwhile, the six or seven women in line leaned forward to see what the commotion was about.

Everything after that was a blur of fear, embarrassment and self-hatred for heeding Nature's call. I couldn't get out of the room. More and more people gathered around the opening. Shouts and laughter were coming from all directions.

"Mary? Mary!" I frantically looked, but she was gone.

"Pervert!" women's voices called out, followed by blows. A woman soon came in followed by a uniformed security guard.

"It's time to go," he announced, and I couldn't have agreed more. I breathed a sigh of relief. But as I finally broke free and turned to rejoin my friends, a hand on my arm stopped me. Before I knew it, I was dragged out of the bar and handcuffed by an actual police officer.

"I'm a girl!" I repeated desperately. "This is a mistake." The officer refused to listen or look at my ID. I tried to reach for it in my back pocket, but the handcuffs thwarted my attempts. I looked out into a crowd that had instantly gathered around us. Finally, after what felt like an eternity, I spotted a face I recognized. Mary came running up.

"What did you do?" she asked, alarmed. After a confused exchange between the three of us, the officer realized there had been a misunderstanding and released me. We tried to go back inside together, but the officer stood between the door and me.

"You're banned for making a disturbance," the security guard informed me stoically. I couldn't believe the nightmare wasn't over. I tried to call my other friends to tell them what happened, but it was loud inside and their phones went unanswered.

"I'll go inside and get them," Mary offered kindly. I shoved my phone back into my pocket and sighed.

"No, you go back in and have fun." She smiled slowly and nodded. I knew she would make up some excuse for my early departure.

I walked home alone, grateful that my humiliation wouldn't become public knowledge. The longer I trudged along though, the more I couldn't forget the feeling of stepping out of that bathroom stall and seeing only the faces of strangers.

"I hate you, Mary," I thought. "No, I hate myself." Though I wanted to cry, I couldn't. I hadn't cried since I was a child.

After that night, I finally heard what the universe was trying to tell me. I had been confused before—it was when I was presenting as a girl that I was pretending, not the other way around. I crossed the line and never looked back.

PRIVILEGE:

I SEEM TO HAVE IT, NOW WHAT?

lore m. dickey

Shortly after beginning my own transition, I was hanging out with a bunch of friends when one of the guys, a white trans man, jokingly quipped: "I keep waiting for the male privilege to show up." We all laughed; it seemed funny at the time.

The more I've thought about it over the last fourteen years however, the less humorous and more complicated it has become. Through lived experience and conducting workshops on gender, I've come to understand that male privilege is a *complex* subject. Its effects depend on context and the people with whom I'm interacting—they're real, but unpredictable. Then again, I've learned that being a man isn't *just* about having privilege. I've also experienced certain downsides of being a man with a trans history in American society.

Bathrooms have never been a safe place for me. As a child, this was simply a source of confusion; as a man, I still can't quite let my guard down. The first thirty-seven years of my life I tried to fit into a world where my femaleness felt out of place. The first time I became aware of this, I was only eight-years-old, dressed in my green Girl Scout uniform, entering the restroom at a public hockey arena.

"You know this is the women's restroom?" a middle-aged woman declared as I entered. I felt a moment of panic and froze.

Though I knew I was in the right place, I didn't feel I had the right to put an adult in her place. Since then, I have never responded directly to people who've questioned my presence in a restroom. I kept the snappy responses that I wanted to make to myself instead.

The last time I had a chance to consider using one, I was nearly assaulted by the father of a young girl. As I exited the restaurant's bathroom with a friend, he was waiting outside with his arms across his chest and his face contorted in anger.

"You know this is the women's restroom?" he demanded.

Accustomed to this response, I hastily passed him without a word. My friends, worried for my safety, decided we should leave.

Nowadays, I can use the men's room uneventfully. No one has ever used the "wrong" pronouns with me since I started transitioning. I am 5'9", have a round belly and my graying hair is thinning. Nothing about my appearance would lead a person to think I have a female past.

Whenever I do come out to people about my trans history—which usually happens within two or three interactions—I often receive reactions of disbelief. A common refrain is: "I would have never known!"

Instantly, I am glad that they see me simply as a man. Then I think of the people who don't have the same "passing" privilege as I—that ability to walk around without my trans history exposed, allowing me the choice of when to disclose. While I find the entire concept of "passing" problematic, I know I benefit from it.

As a child, I lived in a 3,000+ square foot family home and was afforded access to anything I might have wanted. I was raised upper-middle class in a European-American family in Phoenix, Arizona. I attended camp every summer and participated in after-school sports. There was always a hot meal on the table, a roof over my head and the opportunity to participate in community activities.

My sheltered upbringing prevented me from exposure to people who struggle to make ends meet. My first experience with people from various socioeconomic backgrounds occurred in a diversity training workshop sponsored by the Girl Scouts. Twenty participants gathered in a room at a local community college that I had attended several years earlier.

We all sat in plastic chairs that became uncomfortable after a half hour. It was a relief when our instructor finally asked us to stand.

"Line up according to the socioeconomic class in which you were raised." We shuffled around the room, and it quickly became clear that I was an outlier. Most of the other participants clumped near the "working class" end of the spectrum. I suddenly felt as though I didn't belong—not because I didn't have anything to offer, but because others probably didn't want me to participate any longer. I wondered if they thought my family history meant I couldn't understand or relate to marginalized experiences. As the activity came to a close, I felt exposed. I wished I had been dishonest about my background and vowed to keep that information to myself in the future.

Today, nearly twenty years later, I talk about my background a lot more. Still, I worry that others will receive an impression of me that isn't accurate as to how I currently live.

It's certainly true that my background impacts the ways I look at the world. Growing up, I realize I had no sense of whose family was "better off" than others, that whenever something broke or stopped working we simply got a new one. However, it all doesn't change the fact that as I've moved through adulthood, I've had opportunities to learn firsthand how difficult it is to get ahead, especially when parts of my identity have worked against me.

———

One morning in my third year working in the office of a public utility company, a co-worker answered the "employee concerns" hotline. Someone who worked for our company had called to complain about the existence of a new LGBT employee resource group. My co-worker, a straight, cisgender man, thought it would be humorous to have me, an out lesbian, respond to the call. So he forwarded it to my voicemail and waited.

As I listened to the message several hours later, he and another male co-worker peered over the gray cubicle wall, eagerly awaiting my reaction. As they laughed, I felt the blood rush out of my face. I slammed down the phone, rushed out to the elevators and insistently pressed the button. What seemed like a careless prank to a person who had privilege was very damaging to a person with a marginalized identity.

I had to talk to someone who could understand and I was fortunate to find a sympathetic shoulder in the employment non-discrimination office. It happened that the head of the EEO was one of the other out lesbians in our workplace. Appalled by the incident, she encouraged me to take the rest of the day off.

There was no way for me to know if or how my coworkers were disciplined, but it didn't matter, because I made every effort to avoid interacting with them for the remainder of my employment there. As far as I knew, they never saw anything wrong with what they did, nor the need to apologize. When our respective roles required we work together, all I could think was: *If it was appropriate, in their minds, for me to respond to this bigoted coworker, what else would they do?* I never felt safe with them again.

After transitioning—and many years since those troublesome coworkers had left—I decided to return to the public utility company. At the time, I had been working in a manufacturing job where I felt unsafe being out as a trans man; I needed a workplace where my boss would be well aware of my transition status.

After about six months back at the office, my manager called me into her office to discuss changing the focus of my role as a Public Relations Specialist; the change would also entail a salary increase. Given my history with this employer, I had expected the same experience of asking for promotions and being denied. Over the next four years, however, I was promoted several times, eventually becoming a Senior Business Analyst.

By the time I left to return to graduate school, my pay had almost doubled. While it is impossible to know all of what led to that series of advancements, I can't help but sense it had something to do with my being a man.

This experience of employment advancement was actually exceptional for me. As I moved through male adulthood financially independent of my parents, I have mostly struggled to make ends meet. At times I have had to live on public assistance.

I acknowledge that this is not the same experience as those who work one or multiple minimum-wage jobs, as those who find it difficult to do much more than survive. Even so, my ability to advance in life is the result of multiple factors that include, but also go beyond, gender.

For instance, I've chosen to live alone, single and childless for the last fifteen years. While this means that I have fewer monthly expenses, I'm still responsible for all the household costs that are usually shared between roommates. At the end of the month I am typically holding my breath until my next paycheck comes.

———

I was enrolled in a graduate program at the Leadership Institute of Seattle and a member of an LGBT community chorus when I decided to transition. A new member had joined the chorus; when he talked about his transition from female-to-male over breakfast at the annual retreat, I felt as though he was describing *my* life. Suddenly, I was facing the challenge of balancing my personal need for chest reconstruction with the academic burden of a major term paper.

I made an uncharacteristic decision: *I'll put myself first even if it means that I won't graduate on time.*

Only halfway done with my degree and in the midst of transition, I realized I wasn't emotionally ready to complete school. Though as a child I had been taught that other people always come first, I could only get what I needed by prioritizing my own needs. I gave myself time to create a colorful brochure seeking financial support for chest reconstruction. I spent hours developing the story of my decision to transition.

In the end, though, my mother, siblings, aunts, uncles, and cousins all chose not to support my surgery. Instead, my friends pitched in, coming up with 70% of the nearly $7,000 cost. I had been doing odd jobs part-time, including two hours a day as a city bus driver. I did have health insurance and was paid a decent hourly wage, but it had been impossible to save because I could only work ten hours a week. Thus, while I came from a socioeconomically privileged background, I found that, like many trans people, it was nearly impossible to afford medical care without the help of friends.

Around this time, I began to ruminate about my safety as a trans man. I wondered: *What would happen to me if I had a medical emergency and was unable to speak for my needs? What if someone discovered that my genitals did not match my outward gender expression?*

Walking down the streets of Seattle prior to transition, I had never felt a concern for my safety. Although I was cautious, I went wherever I wanted at any time of day. Not until I began transitioning did I feel unsafe knowing that men are much more likely to hurt a male stranger if they feel threatened.

I am fortunate—likely due in part to my passing privilege, neighborhood and lack of using public transport at night—that I've never been assaulted either verbally or physically since transitioning. Still, I'm very aware of my surroundings and if I need to be out after dark I make sure I know where I'm going or am surrounded by others. I don't make eye contact with people I don't know, and, if I feel threatened, I walk away.

I didn't have an opportunity to discuss this issue until the FORGE conference in Milwaukee, Wisconsin in 2007.[1] I facilitated a workshop entitled, "Male Privilege and the FTM," and explored numerous questions: *What does it mean to have white male privilege? Should I seek this out as a trans man? How should I respond when someone implies that I am the beneficiary of white male privilege? If I become defensive, does this prove their point? How can I engage in a conversation without being seen as defensive? Do I have the right to defend my position?* I began by modifying Peggy MacIntosh's well-known exercise, "White Privilege: Unpacking the Invisible Knapsack," and the conversation progressed organically from there.

To answer those questions effectively, I strove to understand my trans brothers' unique experiences, being especially aware that my own as a white trans man were different from trans men of color and migrant men. I asked men of color to speak from their own experiences so that I, and others, could understand how their lives have been affected by a complex intersection of privilege and discrimination, hate messages and exclusionary practices. I've heard from many men that, like me, they feel unable to fully escape their trans histories, or are seen as more threatening now that they are male. For example, when I fill out job applications, I worry that my previous name and gender will come back to haunt me. If I list my old name, I may not get an interview at all. But if I do not answer truthfully to avoid discrimination, then I risk being fired for lying on the application and being trans.

One of the most important things I've learned since transitioning and listening to my peers is that becoming men does not automatically or categorically *improve* our social status or lives. Further, many trans men don't have the class or citizenship privileges that I've had, and thus may not have access to healthcare, education or other social opportunities, like safe and affordable housing.

Listening to other trans men's diverse experiences gives me insight into the complexity of trans men and power relations in our society. Whenever possible, I make a conscious effort to use my privilege to support those who do not share my racial, class, and gender advantages.

TRANSMAN ON THE QUEST FOR HAPPINESS

Ryan K. Sallans

Is there a point in transition where one reaches pure happiness? It is a question that I am frequently asked by anxious individuals who are considering or have already started their transition. It is a question I am frequently asked by concerned family members and friends who want their child, sibling or partner to finally feel peace within their body. It is a question asked by ambitious professionals who serve the transgender community, professionals who are seeking knowledge and those key points that will make them better providers. It is a question that I ask myself—and one that I cannot concretely answer.

We'd all like to think that when one transitions they will reach a point where they feel whole, at peace and satisfied with both their internal and external layers. I am now eight years into my transition, I've completed all the surgeries, I am married and I run a successful business, but I struggle with depression and moments where I know being transgender leaves me with some genetic barriers.

My struggle with depression makes me wonder if happiness can drive out the pain and, if so, how does it happen and how is it measured? Do you just wake up one morning and swing your feet out of bed, place them on the ground and then say, "Wow, I am happy. I am content"? Is it brought to you after an amazing orgasm where you lay naked and sweaty next to your partner and have a euthanizing warmth rush through your core and out to your limbs, numbing the pain and bringing forth the pleasure? Or is it that one moment where you look in the mirror and don't have the urge to either put on clothes or cover up with a towel and just think, *Okay, I am happy...?*

After completing several stages in my life where I think I have hit the point where I think I will finally be happy, other emotions—fear, anxiety, depression or anger—pull me away. I am now learning that happiness cannot be measured by where someone is in their transition; in fact, transition has very little to do with it.

———

My eyes burn, the salt searing through my membranes quicker and more aggressively than I remember from my childhood. People say that we become less tolerant of pain as we age, but at thirty-three I didn't think I should be *this* less tolerant. I take my hands, wet with the same salty water that just hit me dead on from the unpredictable waves of the Atlantic Ocean, and rub my eyes. I hope this will help ease the stinging sensation, but it only makes it worse.

I haven't been body surfing since I was eighteen. I actually haven't been in an ocean at all for the past fifteen years. The way the waves push me around, lift me up and tumble me down makes me feel small, yet mighty at the same time. I'm on the tumble setting of the washing machine and loving the youthful bliss that runs through me with each shift in the water's pattern.

Lily, my fiancée of three weeks, is the one who has pulled me out into the ocean at five o'clock this evening. She is the one who makes me forget, or at least ease up, on my adult brain's rationales: a *shark's prime feeding time being between five to seven at night, which increases a person's risk of being attacked.* Being out in the waves with her, hearing her laughter—it's all reminded me what living is supposed to be about. It isn't about fear. It isn't about the most rational approach. And it certainly isn't always about me evaluating myself and my transgender identity.

Suddenly being in the ocean during a shark's prime feeding time turns into just...fun. Time, dates, age, body parts being seen by others, identity, names—none of it matters. We're having fun. Without using time as a reference, we stay out in the water until the chills start to permeate our skin and harden our joints. "Race you to the beach!" Lily yells as her lanky arms start a windmill motion and her stilt-like legs start to kick through the water.

I ignore the fact that she has just gotten a head start and don't let gender dictate who should or shouldn't win the race. I began to charge my more stocky build ahead of her, memories of my teenage years and the hours upon hours I would spend swimming, racing friends in a lap pool or seeing who could hold their breath the longest rush past me, in sync with the water.

"Beat you!" I yell with my camera-caught finish. I shake my head back and forth to keep the water in my hair from dripping down into my eyes.

"No fair. You're stronger," she replies as she gently slicks her dark locks back behind her ears. Her svelte 5'11" frame joins my 5'10" frame as we begin to stomp up the shore, transitioning from the compact surface to loose sand that hitches a ride on our wet feet.

I reach out my hand and hers shoots forward to join us together. It is one of those moments where I joke with her, "If this were a movie, the screen would go blank and show us moments later in a passionate embrace." This will be one of the movie scenes recorded in my mind as a reminder of the moments that—unlike those other movie scenes that fade out, only to fade in on a coffee mug being flung across the room or duct tape down the center of the bed. I know those moments will happen, too, but I try to keep the gushy ones more prominent in my mind.

"Thank you for making me come out tonight," I say.

"I didn't make you do anything, but I'm happy you joined me. I was coming out here with or without you tonight!" She reaches out and jabs me in the side.

We've spent the past week in Atlanta, shut up in a conference hotel for an international conference on transgender healthcare. From Atlanta we boarded another flight to a beach house in Charleston, South Carolina for a little get away. It is a trip that wouldn't have been possible without her stepmom's invitation and one we dearly needed.

Lily and I both work tirelessly in the transgender field and find that our work, combined with my transgender identity, makes us forget that there are things outside of being transgender. Being on that beach, shirtless with only my swim trunks lowly set on my hips and not thinking about my scars or what people think of me is another moment I try to take an internal snapshot of as a reminder that I am more than a transgender man. I am a human who wants what other people want: healthy relationships, laughter and relaxation.

I let go of her hand and grab both of our beach towels. Like a maître d' setting a dinner table, I float them over the sand until they are positioned parallel to each other, running east to west.

"Thank you, sweetie."

"You're welcome," I reply as we both sprawl out and look out toward the endless horizon.

———

The sound of the seagulls mixed with the waves beating the shoreline make me feel as if we are listening to Lily's sound machine—but today I feel serenity from nature's recording, rather than irritation from a manufactured sound bite I'd rather throw out the window.

I lean back on one of my elbows and cross my hairy legs, watching little kids splash in the waves. I'm always amazed at how long they can stay in the water without feeling cold; then again, I've heard that the smaller the surface area, the more compact and warm things are. Parents and other adults are scattered across the beach, sitting in beach chairs with their magazines and coolers nearby. Looking at how they interact with—or sometimes avoid—their children, I begin to wonder what Lily and I would be like that if we could have our own kids.

It is one of those thoughts that brings me back to my transgender identity. Up until that moment I just felt like a guy with his gal enjoying the beach like any other couple, but then the reminder that we can't have a biological child or an "oops" baby snaps me back to the reality that I'm not just "a guy."

My peacefulness turns into sorrow—which is ironic since I don't even want to have kids. Our four-legged fur babies are our children and I'm happy with them. My work schedule as a national speaker and Lily's as a therapist keep us on the road or in an office. We couldn't be parents unless one of us sacrificed a piece of our career: something neither one of us currently wants to volunteer for. So why am I now using my transgender identity as a point of contention toward my happiness?

I know there are plenty of people who can't have kids. While our reason is because I'm trans, others are sterile; some have had an accident or have otherwise lost their reproductive abilities. I realize that I lash out at my trans identity because it is the closest and easiest part to attack.

Far too often I find myself or other people in the community attacking our trans-ness as the reason or cause of discomfort or shame when really it is because we don't want to go deeper and understand the true cause of our emotions. Some people may respond to that and say, "Yeah, Ryan, but you've had surgery and you've gotten your documents changed, so you don't know what it is like." But the reality is, I do. In order to get to point B, I had to start at point A. And as a person that is now at point B, I can say the same feelings follow you no matter where you are at. The same excuses, the same insecurities, the same disappointments.

Every day I am learning that we cannot base our happiness on our external appearance or internal abilities. I am learning that we can't find happiness when we focus on what it is we can't genetically change.

Just like this moment, in which I'm lying on a beach with a beautiful woman who has said, "Yes," to my marriage proposal. Here I am, in my swimming trunks, shirtless and covered in body hair from head to toe. I am a guy who has it all, but "having it all" doesn't matter when I choose to focus on what it is that I don't or cannot have.

"What are you thinking?" Lily asks, pulling me back to the present.

"Huh?" I look over and notice her hair is beginning to change from sleek and smooth to frizzy curls. "Oh...nothing."

"Come on, tell me."

I shift my focus back to the kids who are now bent over, searching for the perfect seashell.

"I was just wondering what it would be like to have kids and how we would be as parents."

"Do you want kids?" she asks.

"The funny thing is no, I don't...but I wish we at least had the option."

"I get it. It makes me sad, too. But you know if we wanted a kid, we *do* have options."

"I know. I just wish we had the easiest one."

After saying this I realize how ridiculous it sounds. I know plenty of couples joined together with a penis and vulva, with eggs and sperm, who still can't get pregnant or who have to go through countless fertility appointments to make it happen. In reality, that path isn't necessarily the "easiest one."

And I know my envy isn't really about the kids; it's about the fact that I don't have a big penis and I don't have sperm. It is about the fact that I am without something someone else has. This realization makes me feel foolish and selfish. I feel like the British kid in the movie *Charlie and The Chocolate Factory* who states, "But daddy, he has a squirrel that cracks nuts! *I* want a nut-cracking squirrel." No pun intended.

"Sorry, I sound stupid," I mumble.

"I'm not going to lie. It would be nice to have the choice, but it is also nice not having to worry about getting pregnant."

"Kind of a dichotomy, huh?"

"It is..." she replies, reaching over to push my bangs out of my face.

I glance over and smile, then lean over and give her a small peck on the lips. We both lean back. Our gazes lock simultaneously, propelling us back toward each other for a deeper kiss.

The moment is only interrupted when our stomachs begin to rumble and goose bumps prickle our arms and legs. It's time to head back up to the house for the evening. I let her take the lead and find myself placing my slightly larger bare feet inside the footprints she leaves in the sand.

The connection between where Lily has been and where I am going electrifies the bottom of my feet and sends shivers through my limbs. *I am connected with something beautiful.* I need to remember this when I feel the distance between me and life. I need to remember that happiness is just like any other emotion: it embraces us when we aren't seeking it and it leaves before becoming too powerful, turning us into addicts wanting more than what is tolerable. And when one finds it, how they experience happiness depends on what they choose to see, feel and explore.

WHY I'M NOT TRANSGENDER

Max Wolf Valerio

I wrote "Why I'm Not Transgender" in 1998 for a trans-oriented column that appeared in the online magazine Gay.com. *The essay appears to have legs since, fifteen years later, I am still asked about it and it materializes from time to time on a webpage or in an online trans forum. The identity issue addressed in this essay, nearly a manifesto, is still timely and continues to confound, anger and enliven conversations about gender identity as we cruise into the second decade of the new century and millennium. I wouldn't take a word of it back and I feel as though I have never said it better. So, let me allow the work to speak for itself, here, in print, published in this anthology for the first time.*

———

"Transgender" gives me a slightly nauseous feeling—I sense a touchy-feely malevolence lurking. It's a nice, *safe* word that de-sexes and defangs the term "transsexual" just as that other hideous PC euphemism "significant other" de-sexes the hot, sticky, and passionate reality of being someone's lover. I would never want to go to bed with a person called a significant other. It sounds like an AA or therapy word, more of the psychobabble and pop therapy that waters down our passions and homogenizes our intentions.

I have never felt that the word "transgender" describes the very real and vital biological sex change process at the core of transsexuality. Now, this literally de-sexed word (taking the "sex" out of transsexual) has become the umbrella term for all people who transgress or traverse gender boundaries. It is spawning a pantheon of hyphenated identities, a hyperventilation of male and female combinations.

The term was originated by Virginia Prince to describe the male-to-female cross dresser who lived as female most of the time but didn't have sex change surgery or take hormones. Virginia Prince, a dedicated crossdresser, was apparently not too jazzed about transsexuals and openly referred to us as "losers."

Transgender is now used to describe everyone: female-to-male transsexuals, guys who occasionally enjoy wearing a tight-fitting pair of panties, lesbians who paste on bushy mustaches for a wild weekend and even genetic female lesbian femmes with attitude. It has even been suggested that the entire lesbian and gay movement should just call itself the "Transgender Movement" and forget the terms gay and lesbian. After all, the reason that gays and lesbians are oppressed, this line of reasoning contends, is because they transgress the gender boundaries that prevent people of the same sex from getting sexually, erotically or romantically entangled.

I am a transsexual man but I will grudgingly accept the umbrella identification of transgender in order to better communicate or work with others. After all, I'm already in the larger tent of sexual orientation and gender freaks: Queers. Ultimately, it is to our greater benefit if we try to work towards common goals, like equal rights and the benefits of a just and equitable society.

However, I did not change my core gender identity; I changed my biological sex. True, I cannot entirely alter it, but I decisively shifted the rudder of my biology from female to male, most importantly through the use of testosterone, but also through surgery and my unequivocal daily living in the world as a man. I dislike the use of the word transgender because it increasingly lumps me in with any number of other people who might be transgressing gender boundaries, people who might actually have very little in common with me. While I'm not against these people expressing their gender, I do have a real fear: The word transgender has the potential to entirely erase who I am.

Transgender makes my identity a little more palatable to some. Transgender doesn't remind people of the cutting and sewing of flesh during sex change surgery. It doesn't conjure up images of the regular injection of potent hormones that have lowered my voice, altered my distribution of body fat, made my bones more massive and enabled me to grow an Adam's apple. The same testosterone that has sprouted thousands of coarse hairs on my legs, abdomen and face has also created flashing thoughts of women in various sexual positions in my mind at odd hours of the day.

Transgender doesn't conjure my top surgery or the fact that I intend to have a set of large, bull-like balls surgically constructed to fill out my basket. Transgender doesn't connect me decisively to my spiritual ancestors, the other transsexuals of the latter half of the twentieth century who have endured ostracism, loneliness and intensive struggle to transform their bodies and lives.

Transgender ignores the medical aspects of my transition that have enabled me to create my life as a man. I have made use of the medical tools available to me, against all the odds and the voices that told me I couldn't do it—and that I shouldn't want to.

At one time, not so long ago in feminist history, a woman who wore men's clothes was simply called a butch and, after that, a woman-identified woman. That is, if a woman wore what was considered to be a man's suit, it was now a woman's suit and she was a woman-identified woman for wearing it. The theory went that by breaking a gender role boundary, she was situating herself outside the patriarchy—a culture constructed by men to contain the free expression of women's identity. Paradoxically, this act of wearing men's clothing made her more of a "real" woman, than a "male-identified woman" who wore traditionally female clothes. Perhaps that's what Valerie Solanas was thinking when she wrote the line, "I'm so female, I'm subversive," which her alter-ego character utters during her play, "Up Your Ass."[1]

Times change and so does the lens. Many gender transgressors don't even remember this once radically feminist idea put forward by the

Radicalesbians in 1970. Currently, the same subversive woman might identify as a "boi" or an FTM trans butch, simply by wearing that same suit. Today, that act of gender transgression makes her transgender, not a woman-identified woman. At the 2nd Femme Conference, a non-transsexual femme stated that she was transgender since she transgressed gender definitions for feminine women in straight culture by dating women and for lesbians in lesbian culture by looking and dressing feminine. The arena continues to expand even as the lens shifts.

I have no argument or grievance with anyone transgressing any boundary—in fact, I celebrate it. There's nothing I like better than chaos and subversion. However, my very distinct experience as a transsexual person who has undergone a biological transformation in order to live as the sex opposite to the one I was born is in danger of being unheard. If transsexual and transgender become completely equivalent, then subsequently, my identity becomes equivalent to that of this newly declared transgendered genetic nontranssexual femme or the boi-identified lesbian wearing a suit coat. We may or may not have things in common—but these people cannot speak for me.

Although connected with gender expression and rooted in the mystery of gender identity, transsexuality is really about the larger miracle of changing sex. Anne Ogborn, one of my favorite transsexual woman pioneers, pointed out to me that people are never really sure if we transsexuals are flaming radicals and revolutionaries or complete reactionaries. There is an essential and defiant tension in our decision to change our biological sex that defies casual pigeonholing. Are we buying into the binary gender system or transforming the rules altogether by proving that the exact biology of one's birth is not one's ultimate destination or destiny? Take your pick.

For me, the word transgender does not convey enough of the magic and danger associated with the transformation of transsexuals—the fact that we change sex. It's a concept that's far too irrational and far-fetched for many people to grasp. Transsexuality is not only beyond the true and the real, it's beyond the nice and polite. Transgender can be said safely in mixed company. Like that other trend of always substituting "gender" for "sex," the word "transgender" softens and smoothes out the rough edges. It isn't as threatening, but it also has less charge.

Unfortunately, for many who now call themselves FTMs, particularly those who have a lesbian or feminist background, there is often a very palpable shame about becoming a man. *I have become a man.* I have taken on that identity—not boi, not butch trans FTM, not any hyphenated male/female combination—I am a man. Although I use the modifier of transsexual, these two terms do not cancel each other out. I am not only relating the reality of my experience, I am also taking on full responsibility for my decision to change my biological sex. Part of that responsibility is accepting the historical and cultural onus of masculinity.

Stepping off into a parallel dimension that's filled with risky endeavors and vital forces—that's what doing transsexuality is all about. Transgender doesn't even begin to describe it.

DID I ASK FOR THIS?

Lance Cox

I always knew I'd grow up to be a man, but I never expected that I'd grow up to be an activist. I've learned quite a bit about the queer rights movement and have been inspired by those who came before me, but I didn't think that *I* was going to fit that role. And I definitely didn't believe that coming out as transgender during college would force me into activism. Looking back, I'm starting to understand why that happened.

As a child, I knew something about me wasn't quite the same as the rest of my peers—that I felt more comfortable with the gender-based stereotypes placed on young boys regardless of my anatomy. I would walk around the family sign shop wearing jeans, a t-shirt and a hoodie, calling myself "Joey." I threw my hood up to mask what I thought were my feminine traits. I kept my hair short and asked for the "boyish" cut when the hairdresser asked about my sideburns. At age four or five, I would lay awake at night wondering about the logistics of having a child with a female-bodied person—who would carry the baby? Why this even popped into my head when I was young, I have no idea. I do know, however, that I was neither interested in pregnancy nor maternity. As soon as I was able to choose my own Halloween costume, I went from my parents' gender-neutral selections to distinctly masculine ones like Buzz Lightyear, a ninja, Raggedy Andy and Spock.

Similar to a significant portion of the trans* community, I grew up thinking that I was alone in what I felt. As I grew older, I tried to forget about the years when I was free to assert my masculinity—those days when I could "pretend" to be a boy and my family would simply find it cute or silly. Whenever those moments were brought up, I would deny their existence and ask that we never speak of them again. Puberty arrived and it became more and more difficult to assert how I really felt: that I was a boy.

In sixth or seventh grade, my best friend told me he was gay. He and I started talking about sexuality, as did the rest of our peers, and everyone I knew instantly assumed that I was a lesbian. I tried to identify that way, though never naming it as such—I always went with "gay" instead—to no avail. So, I tried pansexual, I tried bisexual, but none of it worked.

Each time I came out as something different, everyone continued to assume that I was solely interested in women. Truthfully, my fourteen-year old self wasn't interested in anything, but I thought I should like girls because the masculine part of me figured that boys should like girls . . . right? I believed the closest I could ever get to being myself was to be in a relationship with someone female-identified. That is, until I found the vocabulary I had been unknowingly searching for.

The exact moment I recognized the word "transgender" as a possible identifier for myself is lost to me, but the memories of watching other trans men documenting their transitions on YouTube will never fade. The archive of changes that these homemade videos presented was life-changing for me—I could see trans men just being themselves, showing what physical progress they had made through hormones or surgeries. I spent countless hours watching their updates from pre-testosterone to three months to six months to a year on T, constantly envisioning what my future could look like. In my eyes, these men looked like me, talked like me and had similar experiences to what I was going through. Most importantly, though, they wanted what I wanted.

While the reality that men like me existed was incredibly validating, I felt simultaneously immobilized. *What was I supposed to do with this new information?* Growing up in a small town, and in an even smaller school, does not make it easy to escape who and what people already think you are. My immediate thought upon recognizing myself as trans* was, "I need to leave and run far away from everyone I've ever known." I started to confide in a few friends, but I had no transgender community to speak of aside from the videos and stories I could find on the internet.

———

During my sophomore year of high school, I started to look for a place to run to. I found an early-admissions college near Boston, applied, was accepted and even received an academic scholarship. When I visited campus, I met my first fellow transman. Seeing him changed everything. I wasn't alone anymore—I had finally met someone, in real life, that knew what I was going through. I fell in love with the school simply because it felt like an opportunity to be myself. In reality, though, it wasn't financially feasible and looking back, I don't think it would have worked out for me anyway—I just wasn't ready to go to college that early.

So, I found myself back in high school, entering my junior year and in my first relationship. My partner wasn't ready to be in a queer relationship, which resulted in something incredibly destructive. I told her multiple times that being with me didn't mean she needed to identify as anything, and eventually I let her know that I identified as male. I left out the fact that I'm also predominantly interested in men, though much later, after we had parted ways romantically, I let her in on that part of me as well.

She quickly became, and continues to be, my most consistent support system, despite how devastating dating her became. Though she now could see me as male, she was still uncomfortable being with me in public and wasn't ready to be perceived as any shade of queer. For months, I kept myself in that situation—one in which the person I was dating lacked pride in being with me.

In addition to an unhealthy relationship, my junior year also saw many sleepless nights clouded by drugs and alcohol. Friday and Saturday evenings were great for parties, but so was every other day of the week. I found that, while I was still physically stuck in my home town, I could escape through substance abuse. It was much easier to drink, smoke weed and forget everything I was dealing with than to confront any of it head on. There were a few encounters with the police, several angry parents and a lot of toxic friendships, but at the time all of that was easier than coming out as transgender.

As I entered my senior year, partying continued to be a constant in my life and I couldn't help but count down the days until I could escape my town, my small-minded classmates and even my family. I decided on an art school in Chicago that I thought would completely fit my needs: it had a diverse curriculum and a supposedly diverse community, with resources for LGBTQ students and several queer events each semester. Beyond that, the fact that Chicago is home to a queer-focused clinic that uses an informed consent model for hormone therapy solidified my choice to move.[1] I hoped that by leaving my hometown, I could get a new start in the city and leave everyone, including my "former self," behind. And, in essence, I succeeded. When I started college, I got the fresh start I was looking for, found allies on campus and off and now have a sizable community of other trans*, queer and allied individuals that love and support me. But at what cost?

This experience hasn't turned out to be everything I expected. When I came to campus, there wasn't a process to get one's preferred name on class rosters, IDs or any other documents. I had to email every administrator and instructor I was going to come into contact with and explain not only what the word "transgender" means, but that I will need them to make a mental note of my name and pronoun preference.

I was frustrated by having to disclose my identity without meeting these people beforehand, but I was also scared. I constantly found myself wondering, *What happens if an instructor disregards my requests and uses an incorrect name or pronoun during class? What will the other students think? Is this safe?* I didn't have the answers and I was terrified—not only that I might be misgendered, but that the other students in the room wouldn't know what that meant and that they would react in a violent way.

At the absolute least, being misgendered in the classroom was a huge distraction. Around week ten, after everyone in my classes had started to get to know each other, I once had an instructor refer to me with female pronouns. I could sense each of the fifteen students in the room take a breath together and time seemed to stop to allow everyone to process what had just happened.

After that, not only were my classmates confused because they knew me as a man, but I became completely closed off; it made learning astonishingly difficult. There were times that I would skip class in order to avoid being put in that situation again.

Gender-inclusive housing wasn't an option for me either and I found myself living with four girls. I ended up spending most of my time outside of my dorm, in study lounges or with friends, and avoided being "home" as much as possible. My roommates would consistently use my preferred name but disregard pronouns, which made me weary of spending time with them or around anyone I hadn't yet met.

Every time I walked up to my apartment door, I began worrying that someone would see me enter it or spot our names on it and wonder why there was a male name among four female ones. *What would happen if someone saw that? Would they ask someone about it? Would they ask* me *about it?*

My first year of college was meant to be a new beginning—a way out of a destructive space. The problem is, as an incoming freshman, I wasn't prepared to embark on a journey of activism or become the face of the trans* rights movement on my campus. Policies should have been in place to accommodate my requests as a transgender student before I ever set foot there. I shouldn't have to be asked time and time again to educate the faculty and staff, regardless of whether or not I would like to do so. Theoretically, I should be able to let my studies come first but the fact is, it doesn't always happen that way.

For some students, entering college may be a time when drugs, alcohol and socializing are their main focus; for others, student organizations and other leadership roles fill that space. For me and other transgender students, activism becomes our main priority *because it has to*. The need for safe, gender-inclusive housing and restrooms, a name change process, inclusive health insurance, and a larger range of queer studies courses is stronger than ever. College is a time of awakening, self-discovery, and growth, but until institutions embrace gender variance, higher education will continue to be as dangerous as elementary, middle and high school can be.

———

As if this wasn't enough, I returned home for a weekend during my first semester and came out to my family. I knew that they had seen it coming because my mother had once asked me, "Why do you dress like Ken instead of Barbie?" At the time I was eight or nine, and had no articulate response to offer.

When I came out at age eighteen, I finally had the language to answer this question, but my parents had even more with which to follow it.

I arrived home on a November afternoon, having become a legal adult two months earlier and feeling as independent as ever. I told my mother that I needed to talk to her alone, so we went to a movie. On the way there, she kept asking what I wanted to talk to her about and couldn't seem to wait until we finished watching the movie, which had been my plan. She kept asking questions until she hit the right one, ranging from, "Do you want to bring someone home?" to queries about drugs, alcohol, money and college life.

Finally, she asked me if I "wanted to change things." I asked for clarification, although I knew exactly what she was saying; when I answered yes, she told me that both she and my father had anticipated this. We went into the theater, watched the movie in silence and got back into the car to drop me off at the Chicago-bound train. Though I had planned on talking to my mom in depth about my identity and then letting her relay everything to my dad, she had other plans. She called him and handed me the phone without giving me much of a choice. That's when the inquisition *really* started.

Most families have questions, of course—as a culture, we lack a general knowledge about trans and queer issues and parents tend to be caught off guard when their children come out to them. My family was different, though. They didn't ask what I meant or why I wanted to transition. They asked why I couldn't wait just a little longer to start hormones. They asked me why I wanted to transition if I liked dating men—why couldn't I just grow my hair out, start wearing make-up and be a straight girl?

It took my parents a long time to understand what I was trying to tell them. I didn't want to transition to be more appealing to anyone other than myself; it had nothing to do with who I was attracted to. Beyond that, I felt a sense of urgency about transitioning medically that didn't make sense to them and had already started the process. This has left me paying for all of my medical expenses, as well as tuition, rent and other costs on my own. For the longest time they used female pronouns and my birth name without any attempt to change, but recently they have started to make a stronger effort.

Today, after finally coming to terms with my trans* identity as well as my sexuality, I have found myself in an incredible place. Sure, I'm working non-stop to pay my bills, both transition-related and other-wise, and I'm always a little worried that someone is going to disclose my identity without my consent in the classroom. But I now choose to tell my story to faculty, staff and students alike to create impactful change on our campus.

In the year that I've been doing this work, a name change process has been put in place, single stall restrooms now have proper, gender-inclusive signage and we are working on safer, trans*-friendly housing. I didn't necessarily seek to be an activist, but I'm not sure that anyone does. Activism comes with a sense of necessity—if my college isn't inclusive enough for me to be fully content, how do I make it so? How will what I do affect those who come after me?

So, did I ask for this? No. Is it fair? Definitely not. Does it take away from my studies and other college experiences? Sometimes. But is it important? Is it rewarding? Absolutely.

JUST LIVING

Micah

I once asked myself, "When will my transition be complete?" After which I questioned the underlying assumption, wondering, "How *can* my transition ever be complete?"

As someone who identifies as non-binary—neither male nor female—this seemed impossible. How could I ever feel like my journey was over if I could never physically, socially or legally attain my goals? I could not even envision what an end state would look like. But I was blind to one particular point: as I changed, my goals would change with me.

Most of my transition has been a series of such moments that just happen: a careful sequence of orchestrated moves interspersed with luck-of-the-draw, right-place-right-time kind of circumstances. Even the ones that are planned usually have fortuitous beginnings. When I first stumbled upon "transgender"—as a word, as an identity, as a concept that embodied my experience—I did not yet conceive of what I could *do* about it. My dreams of becoming "myself" were intangible and abstract; everything that has taken me there was not yet in the realm of known possibilities.

Everything I've done with my body, from top surgery to gradual low-dose testosterone to a hysterectomy, was, at some point, a new discovery. But even after I'd somehow find out that people underwent these procedures in the first place, a phase of intensive research would necessarily follow, as I not only had to determine how to access these services when my non-binary identity "disqualified" me, but where each would fit into my gender goals. In 2010, official transgender health care policies were on the brink of change yet they still omitted any mention of people not fitting into a gender binary.[1] Chest "masculinization" surgery was contingent upon having initiated or having intents to initiate hormone replacement therapy and obtaining a psychologists' letter affirming my desire to live fully as a man.

On principle, I refused to see a therapist for the sole purpose of obtaining permission for a surgery deemed "elective and cosmetic" by my insurance, equivalent to the breast augmentations millions of others undergo by signing a simple consent form. Part of me was also scared that no therapist would allow me to break the rules without pretending to be someone I was not. As for hormones, those were adamantly on my "BIG NO" list (although I later reexamined that). Above all, I had to honor my true self, as that had been compromised for too long already.

The irony is that I learned about all these requirements only after meeting the first person I could see myself in at my first Philadelphia Trans Health Conference, merely a week before my cross-country move from Philadelphia to San Francisco. This person had gotten top surgery without any intention of taking testosterone or identifying as male. In that moment I resolved to do the same. It was the first time I'd ever heard that people could actually remove their breasts because they *wanted* to. Only afterwards, when I realized how this pivotal moment had changed my life for the better, did I acknowledge how much I had *needed* to.

———

Before my first surgery, I firmly believed that I would be done with transitioning: my gender woes would be fixed for good! Instead, I had opened Pandora's Box and in the weeks following my initial trip to the OR my transition began to take off. I started to agonize over pronouns.

Instinctively, I knew that avoiding gendered pronouns altogether would make me *most* comfortable. But in practice, adopting gender-neutral pronouns takes work. Most people are unfamiliar with how to use them, or refuse to do so altogether. It requires an active and continual "coming out," informing and reminding every single person every single time of your unusual pronouns, a process for which the thought alone was daunting. *Would I be ridiculed for such a decision? Would anyone respect my choice? Was it just too much trouble for too little gain?*

But silently remaining in the status quo proved unbearable. Once I knew I could do something to change it, each "she" gradually piled on top of the other, grating on my carefully constructed new self until I was ready to explode. "There's always 'he,'" I would think. "A simple one letter shift *could* be the solution. But is it?" I didn't feel like a he and I didn't look like one either. I'd go back and forth through all the possibilities, anxiously looping through the pro's and con's of each. This became a theme for the next few years.

Meanwhile, I delved further into other facets of transition. If a person can change their pronouns, they can certainly change their name. And my name, tied to a crumbling feminine past, had really started to bother me. My temporary nickname was just that: a substitute, a stand-in for the word that was to define the new me.

Unsuccessfully I tried on a few others, but all of them proved awkward, as ill-fitting as some of my former body parts. Desperation seeped in—perhaps not only due to this one magical word that eluded me, but because everything about me was changing too quickly. In trying to find my name, my identity, I had lost all sense of self.

Eventually I stumbled upon the perfect name. It had everything I wanted in my new identity: uniquely fresh, androgynously masculine, similar enough to remain subtly tied to my past. A part of me was immediately sure this was *it*, so I quickly made it official.

Within a few days I had changed my name on pretty much everything I could, from my email to Facebook to my Netflix account. I printed out the paperwork for a court-ordered name and gender change (which I had recently found out I could do even as a non-U.S. citizen). Ironically, I had always been more confident in my decision to legally declare myself capital-M Male than in being referred to as one by my friends. I suppose it's my small way of standing up to the system, exposing the ridiculousness of the binary by legally moving from one box to another as I please.

———

It seems illogical to declare myself "post-transition" when I'm still in the middle of everything. My name and pronoun switch has yet to catch up with everyone I know; it's been barely six months after my latest surgery; my new driver's license only arrived a few weeks ago. I've also been dealing with the harrowing process of changing the legal sex on my Mexican birth certificate, which is still in progress nine months after I've begun. My experiments with testosterone are ongoing, having stopped and started my hormone regimen at least four times. No... five. Six? I continue to oscillate between moments when I want to keep inching closer towards "masculine" and those when I want to stop, to just remain comfortably as I am.

I've come a long way in just under three years, but I'm still not "there" yet. So why do I feel done? Nowadays, wrapping up the loose ends seems more of an exercise in paperwork than self-reflection. I'm much more sure now of the path I'm taking. I feel I've made not only tremendous progress, but that I'm certainly closer to the finish. What that looks like I still don't know, but—as with everything in life—nobody knows.

Then there's the transitioning that happens *after* you transition. Whether it's the ongoing reservations about disclosure, changing yet another legal document, or just bumping into an old friend, it is never-ending. People are in constant flux. We age, we grow, we buy clothes, we change jobs, we move houses, we make families. Time is tricky, because that moment that was now is already gone.

As I envision the person I'll become in five, ten, twenty-five or even forty-five years, I'm certain everything about me will change, including my gender: how I feel about it, how I look, how others see me. Being trans is a lifelong condition, just another part of being human. I think I've figured out where I want my gender to be in five, ten or twenty-five years. In this dual reality, I take my time to enjoy the present, while eyeing my future in the distance, keeping it on hold.

I feel a close affinity to older trans men—those significantly older in age, not just in "transition years." I guess I see my future self in them, these men who once tried very hard to be "women." Or at least pretended to try, the battle secretly written on their faces. Part admiration, part identification. We compare scars, internal and external. They warmly welcome me as their younger brother, endearingly dub me "little bear." They've marked the trail so I can have an easier time finding my way. But they can't do the walking for me.

I'm content to move towards that with a purposeful slowness. Older me will be a loving spouse, hopefully be a parent, perhaps even a dad; I'll still be a caring partner, a difficult child, a loyal friend, enjoying whatever-my-job-is that day. As reluctant as I am to relinquish the title, at some point I won't look half my age any more. And as much as I'd like to say I'm a boy, I know far too much for that to be so. Yet I simply don't feel like a *man*.

Gender is fuzzy, inexplicable. Like fish in water, people don't necessarily think about gender or even realize it's there, until it's taken away and they can no longer breathe. When I'm alone or with my partner, my gender floats in zero-gravity, weightless. Gender has become a word I repeated one too many times that it stopped making sense. I've been drenched in it for far too long. But now I'm on the other side, no longer rushing to find that next step in my transition. I'm just living.

AFTERWORD

Daisy Hernández

A couple of years ago, a women's studies professor invited me to talk about feminism at her college. I wasn't surprised when a jock about six feet tall walked into the auditorium and sat in the center row. These lectures are often obligatory for students. Attendance is usually a part of their class grade and that's how I get a chance to address football players and theater majors and the five or seven students who actually identify as feminists and want to be there with me.

No sweat, I thought when I saw the white boy in the center row. I prided myself on being a feminist, a bi woman, a woman of color, a journalist. I knew his type. He had a baseball cap and sat with his legs spread. When the other fifty or so students laughed during my talk, he didn't crack a smile. He didn't look bored either, just slightly blank-faced and uninterested. The moment the talk was over, he would probably either argue that I was describing women as victims or he would walk out with his buddies. I missed one detail: he hadn't come with his buddies. He was alone.

The question-and-answer session began. He was still in the center row with his legs spread and he was the first student to raise a hand. I braced myself. He still had on his baseball cap. He sat up and said, "I like what you had to say. I was afraid to come tonight. I talked about it with my friends, because I didn't know if it was going to be okay for me to be here, if I was going to be accepted..." He didn't disclose if he was cisgender or trans, or if he had another experience, but he went on to share that he was new to all these ideas about feminism and that he was, in fact, interested.

Reading this anthology reminded me of that young man and all the assumptions I made about him that evening. I didn't usually think of myself as someone who pigeon-holed men, but like all of us, I have been trained by my community and church (and also by television programs and government policies) on how to read masculinity and how to do so along racial and socioeconomic lines. White boy in baseball cap? Jock. Black boy in baseball cap? Thug.

When I first dated a trans man it was 1999, and I wondered about how to "man him up." My boyfriend was short with a pear-shaped body and he didn't consistently pass on the street. *Maybe*, I thought back then, *he needed a baseball cap or baggier jeans*. I fell for the illusion that I could keep him safe with an article of clothing, with imposing on him a constricting version of masculinity. I didn't share my ideas with him though, because I didn't want him to think that he wasn't man enough.

Each story in this anthology has reminded me that masculinity is like land, like race, like femininity—its dimensions have been defined for us and that affects trans men and the rest of us, too. As a teenager, for example, I had a boyfriend whose neighbor had to kick her boyfriend out every few months when the caseworker came by the apartment to check on her and the kids. They were an immigrant family and they were trying to get by on food stamps, welfare and his earnings.

Actually, they weren't *trying* to get by. They were trying to do a little better than that and the only way they could do it was by periodically hiding the "man of the house." That was what their children saw and what the rest of us witnessed. Television shows bombarded us with images of men as breadwinners; government policies forced us to disappear the *hombres* we knew. Men in our community, then, were both instability and the longing for stability and these were the roles we expected all boys to step into as they grew up. Likewise, what did we expect of the women in our community? To manage and not expect too much of the men they loved.

232

This anthology is a powerful rewriting of our collective futures. The narratives we were raised on about men are not the ones we need to take with us moving forward. Instead, we have here new stories, new *cuentos*, of men who are "manning up" in the fullest sense of that phrase. They are embracing lifelong journeys to develop their authenticity and complexity as men, fathers, brothers, sons, *tíos* and *compadres*. They are uncovering everything from the sharp edges and solidarity of humor among men to the ways black male bodies continue to be policed. They are learning what is possible and what needs to be challenged. As C. Michael Woodward describes it so succinctly in his story: "I was able to transition from female to male in a matter of months. In contrast, it has taken me years to man up."

The experiences described in these pages are especially significant for those of us who hope to transform the world into a better, more just place. After all, if we want equal work by men and women to mean equal pay and if we envision families staying together and still being supported with a safety net, our ideas of what it means to be a man also have to change. The trans men gathered here are leading the way and the rest of us should take up the challenge to engage with honesty and compassion.

This anthology offers one image I find particularly poignant and that is of the children trans men are raising. I am not referring only to the children who claim a transsexual man as their *papá*, but also to the kids next door and the kids down the street—to every child a trans man comes in contact with as a father figure, a *tío*, a brother, a teacher, a mentor.

An entire generation will be coming of age now with the men in these stories, with a trans movement that is more visible than ever, with these new narratives of masculinities that are as complicated as the men we love. Because a book like this exists, these children have the chance to grow up with a much more generous vision of who they can be and what they can offer their communities. One day then, these children will be writing their own books and assembling their own anthologies about the trans men who shaped the arc of their lives and of a whole generation.

FROM THE COVER:

BJ & THE VISIBLE BODIES PROJECT

"When I was young, I loved reading *Conan the Barbarian*. He was the man; he always got the girl. In my dreams, I was on the horse, saving the princess. What did the girls get to do? They got to be rescued. And that was just not me. Growing up in a multi-racial household, it didn't register that there was any real importance to my ethnicity until the kids at school let me know that I didn't fit in. I was doused by the cold ice water of rejection. As I got older, I became uncomfortably aware of my hair texture, my skin color and my small size.

I felt eroded, frustrated, and angry. I read endlessly to engage my active mind, and escape the painful reality of the outside world. When I realized that the physical envelope that contained my mind could be changed, I began taking testosterone and working out to maximize its effects on my build. I felt like one of Michelangelo's statues, chipping away the unnecessary marble to reveal myself beneath.

One thing I'll never be able to change is my small size. Shrimpy guys need to have mojo to make up for height. I compensate with a hyper-masculine, gothic, metalhead exterior. My style is linked to the holy grail of masculinity: the knight who saves the princess. It challenges the question, am I man enough? I feel comfortable and connected to myself this way, but other people don't always react well to a man who looks like me. I'm never sure how much of the adversity I face is related to my presentation or my ethnicity.

My goal is to reach my idealized self and not let anybody prevent me from achieving that. This journey has forced me to shake some bad habits, like not staying very long at jobs that weren't helping me reach my goal. Being trans forced me to grow out of adolescence fast. My own happiness is at stake and nothing is more valuable."

— BJ, 2013

———

BJ is featured in Visible Bodies: Transgender Narratives Retold, a community art initiative that began in San Diego in 2013. The project is comprised of a series of portraits of members of the trans* community, paired with short written pieces by these individuals. The goal of Visible Bodies is to empower transgender people and educate cisgender people. Production on Visible Bodies: Minneapolis and Visible Bodies: Portland is currently underway. For more information, visit http://visiblebodies.org.

NOTES

THE STONE IN MY SHOE // Ezekiel Reis Burgin
1. Lynda Gaines, "Double Whammy" in Rivka Solomon (Editor), *That Takes Ovaries!: Bold Females and Their Brazen Acts* (New York: Three Rivers, 2002), 51-53.

FAMILY MAN // Aaron H. Devor
1. Rosemary Jones, *Queensland Transgender, Sistergirl, and Gender Diverse Conference*. Web. <http://www.transconference.org.au/invited-speakers.html>. Accessed 23 May 2013.
2. *Zeyda*: Hebrew for "grandfather."

MEN LIKE ME // A. Scott Duane
1. *Metoidioplasty*: a surgical procedure that releases a neo-phallus (the testosterone-enhanced clitoris) by cutting the labial ligaments so that it protrudes further from the body.

NOT A CARICATURE OF MALE PRIVILEGE // Trystan T. Cotten
1. Grada Kilomba, *Plantation Memories: Episodes of Everyday Racism* (Münster: Unrast, 2008).
2. On July 16, 2009, Prof. Henry Louis Gates, Jr. was arrested in front of his house for disorderly conduct. A neighbor had called the police after seeing him entering through a window and assuming he was a burglar.

3. J. Halberstam, "On Pronouns" (3 September 2012), <http://www.jackhalberstam.com/on-pronouns/>, accessed 30 October 2013.

4. By black and brown manhood and masculinities I am referring to the corporealities of men from races, ethnicities and nationalities who don't have the advantages of white skin, linguistic or western geographical privilege.

5. On February 26, 2012, George Zimmerman fatally shot Trayvon Martin, a seventeen-year-old black youth, on a vigilante "neighborhood watch" of his Sanford, Florida gated community. Zimmerman was acquitted of second degree murder and manslaughter charges.

6. Before transitioning I used to think of gender-exclusive spaces as hetero/sexist, misogynist and socially harmful. My views have changed with exposure to them and realizing how important the bonding is to my survival. I see how men enjoy these spaces because they feel freer to express themselves and talk about things that they would never discuss in the presence of women. Women have exclusive social spaces and practices of their own too. Sometimes gender binaries can be socially and psychologically useful. My transition journey is giving me a more nuanced understanding of gender and sexual politics.

FEARFULLY AND WONDERFULLY MADE // H. Adam Ackley

1. In 2013, the American Psychiatric Association depathologized and changed the diagnosis that many transgender people receive from "Gender Identity Disorder" to "Gender Dysphoria." *Diagnostic and Statistical Manual of Mental Disorders, 5th Edition: DSM-5.* American Psychiatric Publishing; 5th edition (May 27, 2013).

2. Michael Coogan (editor), *The New Oxford Annotated Bible with Apocrypha: New Revised Standard Version* (Oxford: Oxford University, 2012), Psalm 139:14.

3. Ibid., *Letter to the Hebrews* 11:1.

4. Ibid., *Exodus* 4:1-13, 6:13, 6:30.

5. Ibid., 1 *John* 3.1-2.

6. Ibid., *Deuteronomy* 1.29-31, 4.37.

WITHOUT LOU, WHO WOULD I BE? // **Brice D. Smith**

1. Susan Stryker, "Portrait of a Transfag Drag Hag as a Young Man: The Activist Career of Louis G. Sullivan," in Kate More and Stephen Whittle (eds.), *Reclaiming Genders: Transsexual Grammars at the Fin de Siècle* (London: Cassell, 1999), 62-82.

2. Louis Graydon Sullivan, *From Female to Male: The Life of Jack Bee Garland* (Boston: Alyson Books, 1990).

3. Stryker's subsequent projects, such as the book *Transgender History* and the film *Screaming Queens*, would establish transgender history as its own field of inquiry.

Susan Stryker, *Transgender History* (Berkeley: Seal Press, 2008).

Victor Silverman and Susan Stryker (directors), *Screaming Queens: The Riot at Compton's Cafeteria* (San Francisco: Silverman & Stryker, 2005).

4. Lou Sullivan Diary, 3 October 1979, box 1 folder 11, Louis Graydon Sullivan Papers, 91-7, the Gay, Lesbian, Bisexual, Transgender (GLBT) Historical Society.

5. FORGE (For Ourselves Reworking Gender Expression) is a nationally recognized organization that was founded in 1994 and is based in Milwaukee. See: forge-forward.org.

NEW TERRITORY // **Jack Sito**

1. *Gender Identity Disorder (GID)*: a term established by the American Psychiatric Association in the Diagnostic and Statistical Manual of Mental Disorders (DSM). GID was formerly used when medically diagnosing what is now called *gender dysphoria* (as of the 2013 publication of the DSM's fifth version

"Gender dysphoria" refers to discomfort with the gender category one is assigned at birth and the gender roles associated with it. It may also entail a physical, "felt" discomfort with one's morphological sex.

PRIVILEGE: I SEEM TO HAVE IT, NOW WHAT? // **lore m. dickey**

1. *FORGE*: See Note 5 under "Without Lou, Who Would I Be?."

2. Peggy McIntosh, "White Privilege: Unpacking the Invisible Knapsack" in M. McGoldrick (editor) *Revisioning Family Therapy: Race, Culture, and Gender in Clinical Practice* (New York, NY: Guilford, 1998), 147-158.

WHY I'M NOT TRANSGENDER // Max Wolf Valerio

1. Valerie Solanas, *Up Your Ass, Or, From the Cradle to the Boat, Or, The Big Suck, Or, Up from the Slime; and A Young Girl's Primer on How to Attain to the Leisure Class* (Scum Books 1967).

DID I ASK FOR THIS? // Lance Cox

1. *Informed Consent Model*: The World Professional Association for Transgender Health first established the international Standards of Care (SOC) for providers working with transgender patients in 1979. The document has evolved to come increasingly in-line with the needs that many trans patients articulate for themselves.

The most recent edition is SOC Version 7, published in 2011. In it, the WPATH updates the pre-transition requirements they had held since the previous edition's publication a decade before. Rather than the formerly required 3-6 months of talk therapy, the current SOC asserts that as long as a trans patient is determined to be in sound mental health, they should be able to access hormones after being informed of all side effects and signing their consent. Should a mental health concern present itself, the patient should be treated, and once stable should still be allowed informed access to hormone therapy. For further information see: Eli Coleman, et al., "Standards of Care for the Health of Transsexual, Transgender, and Gender-Nonconforming People, Version 7," *International Journal of Transgenderism* 13 (2011), 181.

JUST LIVING // Micah

1. The World Professional Association for Transgender Health (WPATH) is an international multi-disciplinary organization. They produce the Standards of Care (SOC), the leading transgender health document, which details best practices for transition.

The SOC's 7th Version (2011) is purposefully vague in regards to references of "target gender" to be inclusive of diverse identities, including those that fall beyond the binary. Moreover, it strongly stresses these are not rules but guidelines, warns against medical providers serving as gatekeepers and allows for flexibility in accessing transition services, emphasizing each person's unique transition and health needs.

Although the newest SOC was officially released in late 2011 (after my first surgery), many medical providers still lag behind these updated practices.

CONTRIBUTOR BIOS

H. Adam Ackley is 47, white ("WASP"), who now lives in Los Angeles, but grew up in Ohio with family roots in Appalachia. Married and divorced twice (in failed attempts to live as a "wife"), Ackley is a gay trans* man single parenting two daughters. Ackley is a writer, speaker, college professor, ordained minister in the historic Christian peace tradition and consultant focused on intersections of faith, spirituality, mental health and LGBTQ issues.

Dustin Ashizz is a physically middle-aged and spiritually adolescent Ashkenazi Jewish guy of pansexual orientation. Raised near New York City, he has lived in many different places, most notably in Jerusalem, Israel. He became deaf at age 26 and uses American Sign Language, yet still loves music as he now perceives it. A former university professor, he is currently a dishwasher and single.

Dr. **Loren Cannon** teaches Philosophy in northern California at Humboldt State University. He finds himself approaching 50 years old and the ten-year anniversary of his decision to transition from female to male. Being white, straight, married, able-bodied and employed has given Loren many privileges which have shaped his perspective. When not teaching and writing, Loren enjoys spending time with his friends and family in the beautiful natural environments of Humboldt County.

James C.K., 29, is never at a loss for words. He is heteroflexible and currently single. An attorney by day, James is a beer snob and karaoke superstar by night. That's not true—he can't actually sing, but he sure does try! James is many things, but most importantly: a son to two pharmacists; a brother to two sisters, both teachers; and a dedicated cat-daddy to three ridiculously spoiled house cats (unemployed).

Lance Cox is a 19-year-old queer trans man from Rockford, Illinois. In 2012, he moved to Chicago to go to Columbia College, where he is studying Cultural Studies and Creative Writing. In addition to this, Lance works with The Self Made Men on their social media team. In his spare time, he enjoys attending live storytelling events and concerts to experience community at its fullest.

Dr. Trystan Theosophus Cotten is an able-bodied black male living post-transition in the Bay Area. He works as a professor, activist and publisher and enjoys traveling around the world lecturing on trans identities and issues. His passion is writing, speaking and serving marginalized groups. Trystan is the Founder & Managing Editor of Transgress Press and Associate Professor of Gender and African American Studies at California State University, Stanislaus.

Aaron H. Devor is the Founder and Academic Director of the world's largest Transgender Archives, a professor of Sociology and former Dean of Graduate Studies at the University of Victoria, Canada. Born in the Bronx in 1951 to Ashkenazi Jewish parents, he has lived in Canada since 1969. He has been with his partner, Lynn, for twenty-four years. They have been married twice by a rabbi, both times as firsts in Conservative Judaism: once as a lesbian marriage, once with Aaron as a straight and out trans man. They have one grown son, a young grandson and a young-adult granddaughter.

lore m. dickey is a 52-year-old white trans man with a lesbian history. He identifies as a gay man. He works as an Assistant Professor of

Counseling Psychology in Louisiana. He is a son, brother and uncle. He is happily single and has been since 1995. He is an activist, scholar, presenter, singer and photographer.

Scott Duane is a 28-year-old white man with a transsexual history. Raised by two atheists in an upper middle class Midwestern family, Scott now lives in the San Francisco Bay Area. He holds a doctorate in mathematics and currently works at an educational technology company designing K-12 math practice software. Scott is queer and can't seem to hide it. He's currently both single and HIV negative.

Nathan Ezekiel, a 35-year-old white Jewish transgender man, lives in Cambridge, Massachusettes, with Angela Gail, his wife of 10 years and their two children, ages seven and four (at time of publication). In addition to being a husband and father, he's a neuroscientist, trumpet player and enthusiastic cargo and family bicyclist. Since 2008, Nathan and his wife have been writing about queer families, non-biological parenthood, donor conception and parenting through transition at *First Time, Second Time* (http://www.firsttimesecondtime.com).

Jamison Green is a 65-year-old male, husband, father, brother and uncle of Celtic and Scandinavian descent from Oakland, California. He is a writer, educator, legal scholar, policy consultant, legislative provocateur, world-traveler and long-distance backpacker. He led FTM International from 1991-1999 and has become one of the world's most influential trans men, impacting the areas of health, law, education and employment policies. His book, *Becoming a Visible Man,* is a leading text on trans men's experiences.

Gus is a white, 34-year-old, blue collar trans man born in the Midwest, who has since lived in a few places further South. Ultimately, he's settled down in the Kansas City area, where he is a family-focused straight man married to a straight woman. They have two kids and are getting ready to try for more.

Daisy Hernández has never been asked to disclose her relationship status in a bio before. At 38, she finds this curious. She will admit to being a Cuban-Colombian American and a bi, cisgender woman of color. She coedited the anthology *Colonize This! Young Women of Color on Today's Feminism* (Seal Press). Her next book, a memoir, *A Cup of Water Under My Bed* (Beacon Press), is forthcoming from Beacon Press soon. A New Jersey native, she has lived in Oakland, California and Miami and now makes home in South Arlington, Virginia. You can read more of her work at www.daisyhernandez.com.

Born and raised in Los Angeles, 47-year-old, **Zander Keig**, MSW, is a differently-abled first-generation Latino man who resides in Berkeley, California with his beautiful and amazing wife, Margaret. Zander is co-editor of the Lambda Literary Finalist *Letters for My Brothers: Transitional Wisdom in Retrospect* and Acquisitions Editor for Transgress Press.

Mitch Kellaway is a queer Latino/white trans man. Now in his mid-20's, he has lived in the Boston-area all his life. He is a freelance writer, editor and independent researcher for feminist and transgender causes, and is working towards becoming an educator. He is a devoted son and brother, loving friend and husband, and eagerly planning his future fatherhood. Mitch is the Assistant Editor for Transgress Press.

A retired teacher, **Shaun LaDue** is a 46-year-old Kaska Dena First Nations trans man living in a Vancouver, BC, Canada low-income housing co-operative. He is single, pansexual and believes in polyamorous relationships. Shaun enjoys writing, acting, making art and being a damn good older brother to younger trans people.

Micah is an awesome little person. At 27 years young, this 5'0" tall white Mexican living in San Francisco, California is also a product designer/developer, partner, dark chocolate lover, rock climber, charming trans* educator and advocate. Blogging http://www.neutrois.me, the namesake of their gender identity, Micah dreams of a world that transcends the binary, where everyone can just be who they are.

Chad Ratner is a 35-year-old Caucasian trans man originally from Palos Verdes, California. He is married to a wonderful woman and they currently reside in Long Beach, California. He is a son and a brother to his supportive parents and sisters. Mr. Ratner is an Alumnus of Queens University of Charlotte, North Carolina He volunteers as both a speaker and writer to educate people about the transgender community.

Ezekiel Reis Burgin is a recent transplant to San Diego. He was raised in a white family with class and educational privilege. He received an MSW from Simmons, which he uses as a counselor and freelance case manager. In his late twenties, he has experienced marriage and divorce. During his life he has been straight, bisexual, gay, lesbian and queer. On any given day he may identify as a man, trans guy, genderqueer or some mix.

Ryan Sallans is a 34-year-old, Caucasian trans man who is happily married to his best friend, confidante and partner-in-crime, Lily. Ryan resides in Omaha, Nebraska but makes his living traveling the nation as a public speaker and author working to break down the myths and misconceptions of what it means to be transgender, both for the general public and people who are part of the community. Honor your truths and maintain your individuality.

Rayees Shah is living happily ever after with his wife in a town somewhere in the northern hemisphere.

Jack Sito is a 36-year-old Chicano FTM who identifies as a straight male. He is currently single and enjoys being in relationships with women. He works as a criminal defense investigator for a law firm. Jack received his J.D. in 2010 and is in the process of passing the California Bar Exam to become an attorney. He is the son of immigrant parents from Mexico City, an older brother and an uncle to his five-year-old nephew.

Brice D. Smith is a 33-year-old white, male-read, queer, out trans man and unconventional teacher. He grew up in the American Southwest and currently lives in Milwaukee, Wisconsin with his spouse and four cats. Brice has worked in academia, labor and finance and looks forward to being a stay-at-home dad. His biography of Lou Sullivan titled, *"Yours in Liberation": The Queer Life of Trans Pioneer Lou Sullivan*, will be published by Transgress Press in 2014.

Emmett Troxel is a 32-year-old transgender man living in Phoenix, Arizona. He lives with his wife of fourteen years, their three dogs and two cats. He works as a data analyst for a financial services firm and is an amateur musician.

Max Wolf Valerio is an iconoclastic poet and writer of mixed race: Blackfoot Indian, (Kainai band) and Hispano with Sephardic Jewish ancestry, who began his medical transition in 1989. He is the author of *The Testosterone Files* (2006), a memoir primarily chronicling his first five years on testosterone and the cultural history of feminism, punk rock and outsider art. Max's essays have appeared in *This Bridge Called My Back* (1981), *This Bridge We Call Home: Radical Visions for Transformation* (2002), *Trans/Love: Radical Sex, Love & Relationships Beyond the Gender Binary* (2011), and *Troubling the Line: Trans and Genderqueer Poetry and Poetics* (2013). His poetry blog is: http://www.hypotenusewolf.wordpress.com. Max is the Marketing & Sales Director for Transgress Press.

Daniel Vena is a white, 20-something-year-old transsexual who still knows he has a lot to learn about being a man, a son, a partner and a storyteller. He looks to both his lovably wacky Italian-Canadian family and his attentive "mangiacake" partner for guidance, support and, most of all, inspiration (for his next creative work).

C.T. Whitley is a 31-year-old, queerly straight, small-statured, pale, blue-eyed, transgender guy living in Michigan. He was born and raised in a working-class family on the Front Range of Colorado. He lost his father as a child. Among many things, he is a husband, son, ally, writer, artist, wanderlust, activist, scholar, former financial officer, consultant, vegan, meditator, animal supporter, environmentalist, sports enthusiast, adventurer, gym rat, Corvette fanatic and free-spirit.

Willy Wilkinson, MPH, is an award-winning writer and public health consultant who helps organizations provide LGBT-inclusive services. He is the recipient of a National Lesbian and Gay Journalists Association excellence in writing award and is the author of the forthcoming book *Born on the Edge of Race and Gender*. Willy lives in Oakland, California with his beautiful, irreverent wife Georgia Kolias and their three small children. For more information, visit http://www.willywilkinson.com.

C. Michael Woodward is a 50-year-old white Euromutt trans man, originally from Indiana. He lives in Tucson, Arizona, with his queer-cis partner Carolyn. If you run into him at a transgender conference, his name badge would be dangling too many ribbons and stickers to see any of them clearly. On any given day, they might include: dude, grad student, queer, bi, friend, poly, educator, writer, advocate, storyteller, lover, brother, kinkster, uncle, son, man and rock star.

Gavin Wyer is a 54-year-old entirely male-identified Canadian trans man who completed a full medical transition over the last two years. As a Jewish gay man, he is interested in how these communities intersect. After taking early retirement from Corrections Saskatchewan, he has relocated to a larger center where he continues to work in the security field. Gavin is actively involved with the transgender community and mentorship is a constant part of his life.

ACKNOWLEDGEMENTS

This anthology wouldn't have been possible without our contributors and readers—thank you immensely for your support.

We'd also like to thank extend our gratitude to: Trystan Cotten, Ethan, Scott, and Max of Transgress Press; Scott, Liat, Wolfgang, BJ, and the whole Visible Bodies crew; Leon Mostovoy for photos; Vanessa Blake for editing; Vanessa and Jesse for assistance with cover design; our advance reviewers; and Jamison Green & Daisy Hernandez for their thoughtful foreword and afterword.

Zander would like to acknowledge his Bay Area trans brothers who provide countless hours of fellowship, the many trans men who agreed to document their lives through film and/or print so that we could all glean from their lived experiences and his masterful co-editor Mitch Kellaway.

Mitch would like to thank Leora James and the Lenn Thrower'83 Memorial Fellowship in Queer Studies for their fiscal support, which helped give him the time to edit.

Thank you Jocelyn, Mom, Owen, Harlan, Christina, and Sara—and too many others to name—for loving me. Thank you Nathan, Jesse, CJ, Alex, Jonah, Jay, Asher, and all the Sunday night guys. Thank you Melanie, Angela, Caroline, Lisa, Jorajana and everyone who has ever supported my writing. Thank you to my educators Frannie, Bob, Caroline, and Karen. Thank you to my faithful teammate Zander.

Thank you to beautiful, diverse members of trans communities everywhere.

CREDITS

An earlier version of "The Glow" by Mitch Kellaway was published in *The Huffington Post* as "Father's Day as a Transgender Man." Reprinted here with permission of the author.

"Why I'm Not Transgender" was previously published by *Gay.com*. Reprinted here with permission of the author.

ABOUT THE EDITORS

Zander Keig is a clinical social worker, FtM community advocate and diversity educator who co-edited the 2011 Lambda Literary Finalist *Letters for My Brothers: Transitional Wisdom in Retrospect.* He lives with his wife in Berkeley, CA.

Photo Credit: Sarah Deragon

Mitch Kellaway is a transgender writer, editor and independent researcher. He holds a degree in gender studies and devotes his energy to feminist, queer and transgender causes. He and his wife live in Somerville, MA, where they enjoy plotting their adorable future family.

Photo Credit: Robyn Ochs

50175458R00154

Made in the USA
Lexington, KY
05 March 2016